Taxcafe.co.uk Tax Guides

Using a Company to Save Tax

By Lee Hadnum LLB ACA CTA

Important Legal Notices:

Taxcafe®
TAX GUIDE - 'Using a Company to Save Tax'

Published by:
Taxcafe UK Limited
67 Milton Road
Kirkcaldy
KY1 1TL
Tel: (0044) 01592 560081

12th Edition, May 2011

ISBN: 978-1-907302-40-4

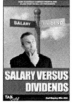

Disclaimer

1. Please note that this publication is intended as **general guidance only** and does NOT constitute accountancy, tax, financial or other professional advice. The author and Taxcafe UK Limited make no representations or warranties with respect to the accuracy or completeness of the contents of this publication and cannot accept any responsibility for any liability, loss or risk, personal or otherwise, which may arise, directly or indirectly, from reliance on information contained in this publication.

2. Please note that tax legislation, the law and practices of government and regulatory authorities (e.g. Revenue & Customs) are constantly changing. Furthermore, your personal circumstances may vary from the general information contained in this tax guide which may not be suitable for your situation. We therefore recommend that for accountancy, tax, financial or other professional advice, you consult a suitably qualified accountant, tax specialist, independent financial adviser, or other professional adviser. Your professional adviser will be able to provide specific advice based on your personal circumstances.

3. This tax guide covers UK taxation mainly and any references to 'tax' or 'taxation' in this tax guide, unless the contrary is expressly stated, are to UK taxation only. Please note that references to the 'UK' do not include the Channel Islands or the Isle of Man. Addressing all foreign tax implications is beyond the scope of this tax guide.

4. Please note that Taxcafe UK Limited has relied wholly upon the expertise of the author in the preparation of the content of this tax guide. The author is not an employee of Taxcafe UK Limited but has been selected by Taxcafe UK Limited using reasonable care and skill to write the content of this tax guide.

5. All persons described in the examples in this guide are entirely fictional characters created specifically for the purposes of this guide. Any similarities to actual persons, living or dead, or to fictional characters created by any other author, are entirely coincidental.

Other Taxcafe guides by the same author

Non-Resident and Offshore Tax Planning

The World's Best Tax Havens

Tax Saving Tactics for Non-Doms

Selling Your Business

The Investor's Tax Bible

BUSINESS TAX SAVER

If you like this tax guide...

You will also like *Business Tax Saver*...

Our monthly guide to BIG business tax savings

<u>You can try it for just £1</u>

Go to www.taxcafe.co.uk/businesstaxsaver.html

About the Author

Lee Hadnum is a key member of the Taxcafe team. Apart from authoring a number of our tax guides, he also provides personalised tax advice through our popular Question & Answer Service, a role he carries out with a great deal of enthusiasm and professionalism.

Lee is a rarity among tax advisers having both legal AND chartered accountancy qualifications. After qualifying as a prize winner in the Institute of Chartered Accountants entrance exams, he went on to become a Chartered Tax Adviser (CTA).

Having worked in Ernst & Young's tax department for a number of years, Lee decided to start his own tax consulting firm, specialising in capital gains tax, inheritance tax and business tax planning. He now provides online guidance and unique tax planning reports at www.wealthprotectionreport.co.uk.

Lee has taken his own advice and now lives overseas himself. Whenever he has spare time Lee enjoys DIY, walking and travelling.

Contents

Chapter 1

Introduction

Using a company could easily save you over £10,000 in tax *every year*...possibly as much as £50,000.

There are several reasons why companies are such powerful tax shelters.

First of all, while sole traders and partnerships pay income tax and national insurance on their profits, companies pay corporation tax – and corporation tax rates are much lower than personal tax rates.

For example, small companies with profits under £300,000 currently pay corporation tax at just 20%. By contrast, sole traders and partners who earn over £42,475 pay 42% income tax and national insurance. Those with income over £150,000 pay 52%.

A company paying tax at just 20% will therefore have a lot more money left over to reinvest and grow than a sole trader or partnership paying tax at 42% or 52%.

Another reason why using a company is so attractive is because, unlike other self-employed people, company owners are in the fortunate position of wearing two caps.

On the one hand, you can reward your hard work as an *employee*; on the other, you can reward your entrepreneurship as a *shareholder*.

As a company employee and shareholder you can split your income into salary and dividends and this could generate large income tax and national insurance savings.

For example, while national insurance is payable on salaries, it is not payable on shareholder dividends.

There are lots of other important tax issues that you have to be aware of when using a company and these are discussed in detail in this guide.

Some of the subjects covered include:

- All tax changes made in the June 2010 emergency Budget and the March 2011 Budget.
- A plain-English guide to how companies are taxed.
- Detailed examples showing the exact amount of tax **you** could save by using a company.
- How to avoid paying any national insurance as a company owner.
- The tax benefits of dividends, plus info on how to pay them correctly and avoid trouble from the taxman.
- How to save thousands more in tax by bringing your spouse or partner into the company.
- The benefits and dangers of owning multiple companies.
- How to incorporate an existing business, including how to make sure you pay zero capital gains tax, VAT, and stamp duty.
- The benefits and drawbacks of using an offshore company.
- A guide to future tax changes.

The guide also contains many useful tables which show the exact tax savings enjoyed by company owners at every profit level. These tables take account of all taxes: income tax, corporation tax, national insurance etc.

There has been much speculation in recent years that the Government would end the significant benefits of incorporation. However, Budgets have come and gone and, while there have been changes, by and large the opportunities to slash your tax bill are still there.

There are also many non-tax reasons why using a company might be a good or even a bad idea. Many of these are listed in the next chapter but they're not the focus of this guide. No other publication focuses on the all-important tax benefits of incorporation, but there are plenty that focus on all the other issues.

It's not always the case that using a company will result in a lower tax bill. There are many occasions when you will be better off owning a business personally. We've therefore included a chapter looking at when running your business as a sole trader or partnership may actually decrease your tax bill.

Chapter 2

Non-Tax Reasons for Using a Company

The most important reason for setting up a company is to save tax. However, there are many other benefits which have nothing to do with cutting your tax bill. Although these are not the focus of this guide, they are worth mentioning in brief:

Limited Liability Protection

In layman's language this means that a company's shareholders are not responsible for the company's debts and cannot be sued by outsiders.

This legal protection comes about because the company and its owners are separate legal entities in the eyes of the law. In legal terms this is often known as the 'veil of incorporation', with the company providing a barrier separating its assets from the shareholder's personal assets.

In practice, much of the limited liability benefit will be taken away by cautious lenders and suppliers. For example, banks will usually not lend your company any money without the directors or shareholders first providing personal guarantees. In fact, many banks make it compulsory to have the personal guarantee concept explained to you by a solicitor... which could cost you hundreds in legal fees.

There are also a number of laws that limit the usefulness of limited liability protection. For example, the wrongful trading legislation effectively states that a director is liable for the debts of a company, where he knows that the company is in a poor financial state yet continues to trade.

Having said this, limited liability protection could prove invaluable, especially if you receive a lawsuit out of the blue or the company goes bankrupt and creditors who did not ask for guarantees are beating at your door. In these circumstances you will owe nothing, except any remaining share capital unpaid.

Given the increasingly litigious climate in the UK, the benefit of limited liability is becoming increasingly important. If this is one of your main reasons for using a company it's important to understand exactly when the courts will ignore the company's separate status and look at your own personal assets to satisfy any company claims.

When Do Courts Pierce the Corporate Veil?

You'll be pleased to know that the general rule is that the separate legal personality of the company should not be broken. There are, however, a number of exceptions to this rule.

The courts can pierce the corporate veil if the company is used:

- For fraud, or
- As a sham to evade contractual or other legal obligations, or
- As a façade to conceal the true facts

However, these 'exceptions' are interpreted pretty narrowly and the courts are keen to preserve company independence.

Where the courts do look through the company to the assets of the shareholders, it will be because the circumstances fall into one of the above categories. They tend to resist any extension of these principles. This was reaffirmed in a case (known as the 'trustor' case) in which the courts needed to determine whether a shareholder, who was the owner and controller of an offshore company, could be held personally liable for the company's debts.

In this case the court said that the shareholder could be held liable because the company had been used as a façade to conceal the true facts. However, the court upheld the strict approach and refused to acknowledge any further exceptions to the basic principles.

Therefore provided you do not use your company for one of the above 'underhand' reasons, the separate legal personality principle will usually be observed.

A common question is whether a company can be used to protect personal assets against a negligence claim. This is important for many professionals, such as lawyers, dentists, IT professionals, and engineers.

To successfully claim negligence a duty of care should exist between the provider of the service and the person suffering the loss.

In order to show that this duty of care was in place, a claimant must usually establish that there was a direct relationship between the claimant and the person providing the service. The claimant must also have relied on the statements made.

This reliance must have been seen to create a 'special relationship' between the director and the claimant (in other words, the director must have taken personal responsibility for the matter and must not merely be acting in the capacity of a manager of the company).

These circumstances where the courts will 'look through' the corporate veil are therefore limited to the established exceptions identified above, and the company can still provide valuable asset protection advantages against creditors generally (provided no personal guarantees have been given).

For detailed advice on the asset protection advantages of a UK limited liability company ensure that you consult a solicitor specializing in this area.

Borrowing Money

It is potentially easier for a company to raise additional finance.

For example, an unincorporated business cannot raise a 'floating charge' over its assets, a company can. (With a floating charge the lender's claim is lodged over a group of assets rather than one specific asset. This leaves the borrower free to sell, buy and vary the assets within the group.)

Equity finance is also available to companies and there are schemes such as the Enterprise Investment Scheme (EIS) that can provide tax relief to the providers of the finance.

Enhanced Status

Trading as a company is often seen as more prestigious than trading in your own name. Many people will have more faith in a business called Joe Bloggs Limited than just plain Joe Bloggs. Of course, it makes virtually no difference in practice whether a business is incorporated or not.

Flexibility of Ownership

Using a company makes it easy to involve new people in the ownership of the business and to separate ownership and management.

For example, if you want to involve your adult children or key employees, all you have to do is issue them some shares.

If you want to keep your stake in the business but do not want to be involved in its day to day management, you can hold on to your shares but resign as an employee.

Similarly, passing the business on to family members can be easier if you use a company as you can leave shares to a number of different beneficiaries.

There are specific tax reliefs available for transferring shares in trading companies (but not investment companies). Therefore if you want to involve younger family members in the business you can frequently transfer shares to them free of UK tax by taking advantage of the various tax reliefs.

Continuity

It's something almost nobody setting up a business thinks about but it's probably the most important decision facing business owners close to retirement: succession.

A company structure allows for a smooth exit from the company.

The death of a company member does not affect the existence of the company. If a partner dies the partnership ceases to exist.

Chapter 3

Company Drawbacks

Using a company is not always in your best interests and it's worth pointing out some of the negative factors:

Costs

It costs virtually nothing to set up a company. All you have to do is go to one of the many company formation experts and they'll do most of the work for not more than £150.

Where you will incur higher costs is in ongoing accountancy fees. Most accountants charge companies more than sole traders and partnerships because of the extra requirement to prepare and file accounts with Companies House. Company accounts need to be filed in a prescribed format and often need to be prepared in accordance with various financial reporting standards. In most cases though, the tax savings should easily cover these extra fees.

Company Law

As a company director you will be subject to UK company law.

Loans to directors are no longer prohibited in the new Companies Act, however there are approval and disclosure requirements unless the loan is less than £10,000.

There are also separate taxation rules that apply an additional tax charge of 25% of the amount of the loan. If the loan is repaid the tax charge is effectively repaid. This is discussed in more detail later in the guide.

Having to undergo annual audits can be an extremely time-consuming and expensive process. However, most small companies no longer have to worry about them.

Generally, a company's accounts will only need to be audited if the company meets one of the following criteria:

- Turnover exceeds £6,5 million per year, or
- Balance sheet value exceeds £3.26 million.

Reporting Requirements

When you operate as a company your annual accounts have to be filed with Companies House. These will reveal financial information about your company. However, small companies only need to file an abbreviated balance sheet. These documents will tell the outside world very little about your dealings.

Accounts must be filed within 9 months of the end of the financial year and there are penalties for late filing.

Company directors are also obliged to keep minutes of directors' meetings, and to comply with statutory filing obligations. Every year an annual return has to be filed with Companies House but, unless there have been significant changes to the company's ownership or structure, this is essentially a 10-minute exercise. There is a small annual filing fee (currently £30, unless you file online in which case it is £15).

PAYE

PAYE applies to any business that has employees and can therefore apply to not just limited companies but also unincorporated businesses. The difference with a company is that, for a sole trader business, the proprietor will not be an employee and therefore not subject to PAYE – rather he or she will be taxed on the profits of the business.

In a limited company setting, the chances are that the directors (previously the sole trader and often a spouse) will also be employees and therefore PAYE would be deducted from any salaries paid to them.

PAYE is essentially a method of paying income tax throughout the year, and the employer company will therefore need to calculate the appropriate income tax and national insurance to deduct from any salary payments and pay this over to Revenue and Customs.

PAYE is usually paid over on a monthly basis: every month you pay the income tax and national insurance for the previous month. However where the monthly income tax and national insurance is less than £1,500, quarterly payments are permitted.

In order to start paying PAYE, the first thing to do is phone Revenue and Customs' new employer helpline: 0845 6 070 143. They will send you a 'starter pack' that explains how PAYE is deducted, along with a variety of forms for you to use.

However, an even better idea is to get a bean-counter to do it for you! There are lots of accountants and payroll firms that will run your payroll for as little as a few pounds per person, per month.

Chapter 4

Why You and the Company Aren't Really Separate

This is the shortest chapter in this guide but the message is an important one.

Although you and your company are separate legal entities, it always amazes us how many authors write about companies and their owner/managers as if they were truly separate. What nonsense!

As a company owner you care very much about how the company's money is spent. It is in reality – no matter what the textbooks say – YOUR money.

As a shareholder you have the ultimate say as to whether it goes to pay for your holiday or is simply given away to charity. Nobody else can tell you what to do with the company's money except in very exceptional circumstances.

In practice, therefore, you and your company are not really separate.

Why are we even mentioning this? Because throughout this guide, when we compare the tax treatment of companies and unincorporated businesses, we are interested in the **whole** picture.

We do not just look at the company's tax position in isolation from you the owner/employee.

We also do not look at your personal tax in isolation from the company's tax bill. We look at both as a single unit. This is the only way to compare doing business through a company with doing business as a sole trader or partnership.

Doing something that decreases your personal tax bill is not much use if it has an adverse effect on the company's tax position. It's your company so in reality the company's tax bill is your tax bill.

Although there are special tax and other laws that affect you and the company differently, ultimately your aim is to use these to best advantage to improve your personal financial position.

There are many detailed examples of tax savings in this guide. Note that all of these examples take into account the tax position of both the company and its owners. So we may be including many taxes in the mix: corporation tax, income tax, capital gains tax and national insurance.

Chapter 5

Company Tax: Pros & Cons

Before taking a detailed look at how companies are taxed and how these special laws can be put to good use to cut your tax bill, it is worth briefly listing the tax benefits of doing business through a company:

The Pros

- Corporation tax rates are generally much lower than income tax rates. For example, a company with profits of up to £300,000 currently pays tax at a rate of just 20%.

- The maximum marginal tax rate for companies is only 27.5%, compared with 52% for sole traders and partnerships (rising to 62% in certain circumstances).

- Company directors can pay themselves a mix of salary and dividends that produces the lowest possible tax bill.

- Further income splitting can be achieved if your spouse is also a shareholder, subject to the settlement rules and any future income shifting rules that may be introduced.

- There is no national insurance payable on your dividends.

- When a company sells assets (e.g. property) it receives Indexation Relief, which eliminates the purely inflationary element of the gain. Individuals do not receive this relief.

- Corporation tax is generally paid nine months after the end of the company's accounting period (although for certain 'large' companies with profits above £1.5 million, payments on account are required during the accounting period). Compare this with income tax which sole traders have to pay twice yearly on 31 January and 31 July.

And the Cons ...

- There is a potential double tax charge if the company sells assets. First, corporation tax has to be paid by the company. Second, income tax may have to be paid by the shareholders if the funds are taken out of the company.

- Sole traders and business partners may qualify for Entrepreneurs Relief when they sell business assets. This means they will pay just 10% capital gains tax. By contrast, a company will pay *at least* 20% corporation tax when it sells assets.

- Having said that, the company's *shareholders* can enjoy Entrepreneurs Relief and pay tax at 10% if they sell their shares in the company, rather than the assets of the business.

- Companies do not enjoy an annual capital gains tax exemption.

- Companies are subject to a separate regime for the taxation of interest.

- Special regulations govern loans to or from the company, which can cause frustration.

- A UK limited liability company is always classed as UK resident for UK tax purposes. As such it is taxed on its worldwide income and gains irrespective of where the shareholders or directors reside (unless a double tax treaty can be used). By contrast, individuals can lose their UK residence by moving overseas. They could then avoid paying UK tax on any overseas trading earnings, whilst a UK company receiving the same income would still be taxed in the UK.

Chapter 6

Corporation Tax in Plain English

The most important difference between the way companies and other businesses are taxed can be summarised as follows:

Sole traders/partners pay <u>income tax</u> on their profits and <u>capital gains tax</u> on their capital gains.

Companies pay <u>corporation tax</u> on both their income and capital gains.

In this section we will show you how corporation tax is calculated. Despite all the mumbo-jumbo in tax textbooks, it's actually quite simple. We will also use a number of examples to compare income tax with corporation tax. The differences are potentially enormous.

6.1 TRADING V INVESTMENT

First of all we must explain the differences between a **trading company** and an **investment company**. There are some key differences in the tax treatment of each. In layman's language, a trading company is a 'regular' business such as a firm of graphic designers or a restaurant or a car dealership. These types of business are the focus of this guide. An investment company is a company that obtains the majority of its income from holding investments such as property.

It can be difficult to distinguish between trading and investment. However, where the business involves passively holding assets, this will be regarded as an investment activity. Common examples of this include a company letting property, receiving dividends or interest from another group company or just otherwise holding assets (for example, holding a cash deposit or holding a patent and receiving royalties).

As we said, this guide focuses on trading companies. Why? Because one of the key tax issues when incorporating an *existing* business

14

is whether capital gains tax can be avoided when the business is transferred into the company. In general only trading activities qualify for capital gains tax deferral on incorporation. An investment activity may result in a significant tax bill.

Note that when you incorporate your business, you will receive a form from Revenue and Customs asking for details of the company (for example, its activities and its accounting period end date) and details of the shareholders.

In addition, you will also have to notify Revenue and Customs within three months of the date you start trading – the date that you start trading is the date your accounting period for tax purposes begins. This will also be the date when the accounting period of your sole trader or partnership business ends.

6.2 CORPORATION TAX RATES

The taxable profits of a company are calculated in a similar way to a sole trader or partnership. The starting point is 'accounting profit' and amounts are then added or subtracted from this figure to calculate taxable profit.

A simple example of how accounting profits differ from taxable profits is in the area of capital expenditure. In the current tax year, which started in April 2011, you can claim a 100% investment allowance for capital spending of up to £100,000. Yet in your accounts you might write off assets over five years, with a 20% allowance in year one. Clearly your taxable profits would then be lower than your accounting profits.

Looking at how those profits are taxed, companies, sole traders and partnerships are all subject to higher tax rates as their profits increase. Corporation tax rates are, however, much lower than income tax rates in many cases.

There are currently two 'official' corporation tax rates:

- Small Profits Rate   20%
- Main Rate   26%

Companies with taxable profits of £300,000 or less pay 20%, and companies with taxable profits exceeding £1.5 million pay 26%.

If profits are between £300,000 and £1.5 million a marginal relief calculation is made. This can be complex but for practical purposes, corporation tax rates can be summarised as follows:

Tax Payable by Companies 1st April 2011 to 31st March 2012	
On the first £300,000 profits	20%
On profits between £300,000 and £1.5 million	27.5%
On profits over £1.5 million	26%

For example, a company with profits of £1,000 will pay £200 in corporation tax. A company with profits of £300,000 will pay £60,000 in corporation tax. Both will pay tax at 20%.

A company with profits of £500,000 will pay 20% tax on the first £300,000 and 27.5% on the remaining £200,000. The total corporation tax bill will be £115,000 and the company's overall effective tax rate will be 23%:

$$£115,000/£500,000 = 23\%$$

A company with profits of £1.5 million will pay 20% tax on the first £300,000 and 27.5% on the remaining £1.2 million. The total corporation tax bill will be £390,000 and the company's overall effective tax rate will be 26%:

$$£390,000/£1,500,000 = 26\%$$

So once profits exceed £1.5 million, you can ignore the 20% and 27.5% tax rates. All profits are taxed at a single rate of 26%.

It doesn't get much easier than this!

6.3   ASSOCIATED COMPANIES

Company owners often think about setting up a second company, to keep a new venture separate from an existing business.

Often there are sound commercial reasons for using more than one company, including to:

- Limit liability
- Involve different shareholders
- Enable a stand-alone sale of the new business

Many taxpayers also ask whether the 26% or 27.5% corporation tax rate can be avoided by simply setting up more than one company, each earning less than £300,000 and each taxed at 20%.

The answer is generally no if both companies are controlled by the same individual. However, it is possible to get your spouse or partner, or some other family member, to set up another company and each company will pay tax at 20% on the first £300,000 of profits, provided the companies do not breach the associated company rules (see below).

The corporation tax profit bands must be divided up if there are any associated companies. So if you own two companies, each company will start paying tax at 27.5% when its profits exceed £150,000 (i.e. £300,000/2).

If you own three companies, this higher rate will kick in at £100,000 (£300,000/3)... and so on. The overall damage is best illustrated with an example.

Example

Jamie owns Company 1 Ltd which has annual profits of £200,000 and a corporation tax bill of £40,000 (£200,000 x 20%). He then also starts trading through Company 2 Ltd.

The two companies are associated so Company 1 Ltd will now pay corporation tax as follows:

$$£150,000 \times 20\% + £50,000 \times 27.5\% = £43,750$$

The company's corporation tax has increased by £3,750.

If Company 2 Ltd hit the ground running and made profits of £150,000 in its first year, Jamie would be no worse off using two companies, as he would still have total profits of £300,000 taxed at 20% (i.e. £150,000 in each company).

However, as long as Company 2 Ltd's profits remain below £150,000, Jamie will be penalised for running two companies.

Loss of Losses

If you expect losses initially from a new business venture then you may also lose out on loss relief if you use a separate associated company.

Example continued

Company 1 Ltd's existing profits are £200,000. Jamie starts a new venture but keeps it in the same company where it makes a loss of £10,000. Company 1 Ltd's tax bill is now:

$$£190,000 \times 20\% = £38,000$$

If the new venture is put in a second company, Company 1 Ltd's tax bill will face a double whammy:

- The associated company penalty
- The inability to offset the loss from the new venture

Company 1 Ltd's tax bill would then be £43,750 – an increase of £5,750!

Note that losses can be relieved where companies are in a group (i.e. one owns the other) but not where they are merely associated (both controlled by the same individual).

What is an Associated Company?

The basic rule is that companies are associated if they are both controlled by the same person:

If you own 51% or more of Company A, you control Company A.

If you own 51% or more of Company B, you control Company B.

The two companies are controlled by the same person and are therefore associated. Each company can only have £150,000 of profits taxed at 20%.

However, if you own 51% or more of Company A but only, say, 49% of Company B you do not control Company B and the two companies are therefore NOT associated and the potentially adverse tax treatment does not apply.

When evaluating whether companies are associated, dormant companies do not count, nor do non trading holding companies.

Foreign companies are included, however.

Family Members and Business Partners

As well as other companies that you control yourself, the law also states that you have to take account of companies controlled by your 'associates', including your:

- Spouse or civil partner
- Close relatives (parents, brothers and sisters, children, etc.)
- Business partners

On the face of it this means that if your sister in South Africa starts a company and doesn't even tell you, you could end up paying an extra £11,250 a year in extra corporation tax.

Fortunately, sanity prevails to some extent and HM Revenue and Customs does not treat companies controlled by any other individual as associated unless there is 'substantial commercial interdependence' between their companies and yours.

Substantial commercial interdependence may exist, for example, if the companies share staff, premises and equipment, co operate on projects or have substantial dealings with each other.

Exception for Unmarried Couples

Lots of couples are not legally married but raise children, start businesses and buy property together.

However, unmarried couples are not recognised by the tax system (with one or two exceptions, eg tax credits). In many cases this is a drawback but it is a big advantage when it comes to running multiple companies.

An unmarried couple can each set up their own company and can benefit from up to £600,000 of profits taxed at 20%, even if there is substantial commercial interdependence between the two companies.

(Note that if an unmarried couple have a separate partnership business they would also be business partners and the associated company rules would apply.)

Companies with Identical Shareholdings

If you form two or more companies with the same shareholdings they will continue to be associated, even if there is not substantial commercial interdependence between them.

Example

Katie and her husband Jamie each own 50% of Company A.

They also each own 50% of Company B.

There is no commercial connection between the two companies but they are associated companies because they are controlled by the same persons.

However, if Katie transfers 1% or more of Company A to Jamie and Jamie transfers 1% or more of company B to Katie they will each control one of the companies – the companies will no longer be controlled by the same people and will not be associated.

Tax Planning Pointers – Associated Companies

- If neither your existing company, nor your new venture, is likely to make profits over £150,000, you may not have to worry about setting up a second company.

- If setting up a new company will result in a higher tax bill, consider running your new business venture out of the same company or as a sole trader or partnership.

- Limited liability for the new venture can be preserved without affecting your existing company's corporation tax bill by using a limited liability partnership (LLP).

- Where a new venture may initially make a loss, it can still be 'ring-fenced' in a separate company without losing loss relief if the new company is owned by your existing company.

Chapter 7

Corporation Tax versus Income Tax

7.1 CASH FLOW BENEFITS

Unlike a company, which is a separate legal entity, all of the profits of a sole trader business are taxed in the hands of the owner (the proprietor).

This is an essential point to grasp. The sole trader will pay tax on the taxable profits of the business, irrespective of the amount that is actually taken out of the business as drawings, to pay for living expenses etc.

As a general rule, a sole trader's tax bill has to be settled by January 31st following the end of the tax year.

A tax year runs from 6th April to the following 5th April. For example, the 2011/12 tax year runs from 6th April 2011 to 5th April 2012.

Your tax return filing date depends on whether you file an electronic or paper return. If you file online you can still file at any time up to 31st January following the end of the tax year. If you want to file a paper return you need to file it by 31st October following the end of the tax year.

For the 2011/12 tax year this means the filing deadlines are:

- Paper return – 31st October 2012
- Electronic return –31st January 2013

In Chapter 5 we briefly outlined the tax pros and cons of using a company. One of the 'pros' is that corporation tax is generally paid nine months *after* the end of the company's accounting period.

In comparison, most sole traders have to make two payments on account – in other words, they have to pay their taxes up front.

Payments on account are based on the income tax liability of the *previous* tax year.

The payments on account will be equal amounts, based on the actual income tax liability of the preceding year, less any tax already deducted at source.

Example

For the 2011/12 tax year Anita, a sole trader, has the following tax bill:

	£
Capital gains tax	10,000
Income tax	35,000
Less: tax deducted at source	-20,000
Net liability	25,000

Payments on account for the 2012/2013 tax year will be as follows:

Income tax	35,000
Tax deducted at source	-20,000
	= 15,000

First payment on account due 31st January 2013 £7,500
Second payment on account due 31st July 2013 £7,500

A balancing payment is also due on 31st January 2014. This will depend on the actual tax liability for 2012/13 (including any capital gains tax liability), less the payments on account that have already been made.

In conclusion, many companies enjoy significant cash flow advantages over many sole traders.

7.2 SELF-EMPLOYED INCOME TAX RATES

Sole traders and partners are subject to the same income tax rates as any salary earner or other personal taxpayer. These can be summarised as follows:

Income up to £100,000

If your income is under £100,000 you will pay income tax at the following rates:

Personal Tax Rates 2011/12 Income up to £100,000	
First £7,475	0%
Next £35,000	20%
£42,475-£100,000	40%

Most sole traders enjoy a tax-free personal allowance which means the first £7,475 of their profits is tax free.

The next £35,000 of profits is subject to basic-rate income tax at 20%.

If you add together £7,475 and £35,000 you get £42,475 – the point where higher-rate income tax at 40% kicks in.

(There is also a 10% savings rate but this only applies to savings income such as bank interest and not to earned income.)

Income between £100,000 and £114,950

Once your income exceeds £100,000 your £7,475 income tax personal allowance is gradually taken away.

It is reduced by £1 for every £2 you earn above £100,000. So once your income reaches £114,950 you will have no personal allowance at all.

This is bad news for those earning over £100,000. The personal allowance currently saves you £2,990 in tax if you are a higher-rate taxpayer.

It doesn't matter what *type* of income you earn. Your personal allowance will be withdrawn if you have savings income, business profits, rental income or employment income.

Example

Bill has earnings of £110,000. His earnings exceed the £100,000 limit by £10,000.

This means his personal allowance will be reduced by half this amount (£5,000), leaving him with a personal allowance of £2,475.

It's important to note that the £5,000 of income that was tax free will now be taxed at 40%, not 20%. The basic-rate tax band is limited to just £35,000 of income.

In summary, Bill pays income tax at the following rates.

First £2,475	0%
Next £35,000	20%
Next £72,525	40%

Paying Tax at 60%

Anyone earning between £100,000 and £114,950 faces a marginal income tax rate of 60%. This can be illustrated with the following example.

Example

Carol earns a salary of £100,000 and pays tax as follows:

	£
Income	100,000
Less: Personal allowance	7,475
Taxable income	92,525
Basic-rate tax £35,000 @ 20%	7,000
Higher-rate tax £57,525 @ 40%	23,010
Total tax	30,010

She receives a pay rise of £10,000 to £110,000. Her income tax personal allowance will be reduced by half this amount (£5,000), leaving her with £2,475.

Her tax bill will now be calculated as follows:

	£
Income	110,000
Less: Personal allowance	2,475
Taxable income	107,525
Basic-rate tax £35,000 @ 20%	7,000
Higher-rate tax £72,525 @ 40%	29,010
Total tax	36,010

Carol's income has risen by £10,000 and her tax bill has risen by £6,000, so her marginal tax rate is 60%.

Income over £114,950

Once you earn over £114,950, you will lose your income tax personal allowance altogether.

When your income goes over £150,000 you will also start paying income tax at 50%. This is known as the 'additional rate'.

Those who earn over £114,950 therefore pay income tax as follows:

Personal Tax Rates 2011/12	
Income over £114,950	
First £35,000	20%
Next £115,000	40%
Over £150,000	50%

Income Tax vs Corporation Tax

So which tax rates are better – the corporation tax ones outlined in the previous chapter or the personal tax rates discussed above? The best way of comparing them is to use some examples.

Let's say Joe Bloggs Limited has taxable profits of £100,000. Put that number into the corporation tax table in Section 6.2 and you will see that the company's tax is only £20,000 (£100,000 x 20%).

But what if Joe Bloggs is a sole trader? Put £100,000 into the above personal income tax table for income up to £100,000 and you will produce a tax bill of £30,010. Joe has saved £10,010 by trading as a company.

Similarly, if Joe Bloggs Limited has profits of £200,000 the company will pay £40,000 in corporation tax. However, if Joe is a sole trader, putting £200,000 into the above personal tax table for income over £114,950, produces a tax bill of £78,000.

The company pays £38,000 less tax than the sole trader!

Table 1 compares corporation tax and income tax at other profit levels. Note that when profits are less than £50,000 income tax is actually lower than corporation tax. The £7,475 personal allowance, available to individuals and not companies, significantly lowers the tax charge.

At profit levels above £50,000 the 40% income tax rate will have already kicked in and a company will start showing its mettle. The lower corporation tax rate begins to offset the higher income tax rate, and the company produces the lower tax charge.

The table also shows the big increases in income tax when profits increase from £100,000 to £120,000 (due to the withdrawal of the personal allowance) and when profits go above £150,000, thanks to the 50% additional tax rate.

Clearly the difference between how companies and individuals are taxed is potentially enormous and it is these potential tax savings that make trading through a company so attractive to many.

For now it's worth stating that: **Corporation tax rates can be much lower than income tax rates.**

TABLE 1
Corporation Tax vs Income Tax 2011/12

Profits £	Corporation tax £	Income tax £	Saving £
10,000	2,000	505	-1,495
15,000	3,500	1,505	-1,495
20,000	4,000	2,505	-1,495
25,000	5,000	3,505	-1,495
30,000	6,000	4,505	-1,495
35,000	7,000	5,505	-1,495
40,000	8,000	6,505	-1,495
50,000	10,000	10,010	10
60,000	12,000	14,010	2,010
70,000	14,000	18,010	4,010
80,000	16,000	22,010	6,010
90,000	18,000	26,010	8,010
100,000	20,000	30,010	10,010
120,000	24,000	41,000	17,000
140,000	28,000	49,000	21,000
160,000	32,000	58,000	26,000
180,000	36,000	68,000	32,000
200,000	40,000	78,000	38,000

There's something else that is not immediately apparent from a cursory examination of Table 1: The tax savings become *proportionately* larger as the profits of the business increase.

The reason for this is that companies with profits below £300,000 pay tax at a flat rate of 20% – the tax rate does not increase as the amount of profit increases. This is a fantastic situation for company owners.

Most tax systems in the Western world are *progressive* – in other words, tax rates go up as profits go up. But in the UK, a company with £300,000 of profits pays tax at the same rate as a company with £1,000 of profits.

What more incentive do you need to grow your business?

With personal tax rates the story is completely different.

As a sole trader, when your business profits exceed £42,475 the extra income you earn is taxed at 40%. When your profits exceed £100,000 your personal allowance is gradually withdrawn and when your profits exceed £150,000 you start paying tax at 50%.

This means your overall effective tax rate goes higher and higher as your profits increase. For example, a sole trader earning £50,000 of profits only pays tax at an overall rate of about 20%; a sole trader earning £200,000 pays tax at an overall rate of 39%.

The important thing to note is that:

As profits go up, using a company becomes more and more attractive.

Although there are clearly massive differences between the tax burdens facing companies and other unincorporated businesses, so far we have not looked at the complete picture. We have been skewing things partly in favour of using a company. Why? Because we have ignored the tax position of the *owners* of the company.

For proprietors or partners of unincorporated businesses there is no further tax liability to worry about once income tax has been paid on the profits of the business.

However, if a company owner wants to get his hands on the company's profits he has to pay himself a dividend or salary. This could lead to more tax being paid.

The critical question is: After paying any extra tax, are you still better off using a company?

Answering this very important question, and showing you how you can structure your pay, is a major focus of the remainder of this guide.

However, before we move on it's important to note that the massive tax savings listed in Table 1 can, in certain circumstances, be realised in practice and put to good use.

To find out how, read on!

7.3   REINVESTING PROFITS

Although extra tax is often payable when profits are withdrawn from a company via a salary or dividend, no extra tax has to be paid if profits are simply *reinvested*.

So the next important point to note is that:

Using a company is attractive if profits are reinvested.

Why reinvest profits? One reason would be to grow your company in order to create a more valuable business that generates even higher income.

The business could then be sold at some point in the future. In these circumstances, the dividend tax problem does not exist because no dividends are being paid!

Selling businesses is probably the most tax-efficient way to make a living in the UK. The proceeds are subject to capital gains tax and, if your company is a 'trading' company (rather than an investment company), you may qualify for Entrepreneurs Relief.

Entrepreneurs Relief allows up to £10 million of capital gains from the sale of businesses during your lifetime to be taxed at just 10%.

Entrepreneurs Relief applies on a per person basis, so couples can have up to £20 million of gains taxed at 10%.

The £10 million limit applies to business sales that take place after 5th April 2011.

In effect, selling a business is a way of converting fully taxed income (future profits, salary, dividends etc) into capital gains that are taxed at a much lower rate.

Even if you decide not to sell your business, reinvesting profits will allow you to earn a higher income in the future, if done wisely.

Again using a company will add a great deal more powder to your keg. A company with £100,000 of profits will have over £10,000 more money left after tax than a sole trader. This money can then be spent on computers or developing new products etc.

A company with £200,000 profits will have around £38,000 more money left after tax.

Of course, it's very unlikely that all of the profits of your business can be reinvested. If you want to pay yourself some income the incorporation question becomes a great deal more complex.

A whole host of factors come into play: national insurance, how much of the company's profit you would need to extract as dividends, the level of the company's profits and the tax-splitting opportunities available to you and your spouse or partner.

We will take a look at each of these factors in turn, starting with national insurance. Before you gulp, there is good news! If you incorporate you may be able to avoid paying national insurance altogether!

Chapter 8

National Insurance Savings

National insurance bills have risen dramatically in recent years with the latest increase having come into effect on 6th April 2011.

Before we describe how company owners can avoid paying too much national insurance, it's worth explaining how the tax works.

The key thing to remember is that national insurance is a tax on 'earned' income. A salary is earned income – it rewards your hard work. Dividends, on the other hand, are not earned income – they reward your entrepreneurship. So salaries, bonuses and the like fall into the national insurance net, dividend payments do not.

As a company owner you will be concerned about not just the national insurance you pay on your personal salary but the national insurance the company has to pay as well. That's the problem: companies *and* their employees pay national insurance on the same income.

If you incorporate, you and the company are likely to be subject to significantly higher national insurance costs *if you take most of your income as salary*.

For the 2011/12 tax year the national insurance rates for company employees are as follows:

- The company will pay class 1 (secondary) national insurance at 13.8% on your salary to the extent that it exceeds the 'earnings threshold'. The earnings threshold for the company is currently £7,072. So if your salary is £57,072 the company pays national insurance on £50,000. The company is, however, allowed a tax deduction for the secondary national insurance it pays.

- As an employee of the company you will pay class 1 (primary) national insurance at 12% on any salary you receive over a £7,225 primary earnings threshold. You have to keep paying 12% national insurance until your salary reaches the 'upper earnings limit', currently £42,475.

- Up until a few years ago your national insurance payments stopped once you reached the upper earnings limit. Not any more! For the 2011/12 tax year, as a company employee, you will pay an additional 2% on your earnings over £42,475.

Example

John earns a salary of £60,000 per year from his company. His national insurance is calculated as follows:

<u>2011/12 Tax Year</u>

Employee – class 1 primary charge:

£42,475 - £7,225 @ 12% = £4,230.00
£60,000 - £42,475 @ 2% = £350.50

Employer – class 1 secondary charge:

£60,000 - £7,072 @ 13.8% = £7,304.06

Total National Insurance   £11,884.56

How does John's position compare with his friend Dave, who earns exactly the same income and is self employed – i.e. an unincorporated business?

Self-employed people have also been hammered by national insurance increases in recent years but they still pay far less national insurance than company owners who take all of their income as salary.

A self-employed individual is required to pay the following national insurance contributions in 2011/12:

- **Class 2** contributions – these are fixed at £2.50 per week. Annual bill, £130.

- **Class 4** contributions – 9% on profits between the earnings threshold and upper earnings limit and 2% on profits above the upper earnings limit.

So on Dave's £60,000 profits the national insurance bill is calculated as follows:

£42,475 - £7,225 @ 9% = £3,172.50
£60,000 - £42,475 @ 2% =   £350.50

Class 4 national insurance = £3,523
Class 2 national insurance = £130

Total national insurance £3,653

There's a massive difference between Dave's and John's national insurance bills.

John the company owner pays £8,231 more national insurance than Dave the sole trader even though they earn the same income!

Clearly, using a company in this way would be a disaster. Dave and John would both pay exactly the same income tax as they both earn the same income. But because they are subject to different national insurance systems, there's a massive difference in their take-home pay. Dave the sole trader is much better off.

Table 2 compares the national insurance payable by a sole trader, a 50:50 partnership and a company and its owner (assuming all the company's profits are extracted as salary). At every level of profit the unincorporated businesses are paying less national insurance than the company owner... much less.

This leads us to conclude that: **Using a company is a bad idea when all income is taken as salary.**

TABLE 2
National Insurance Bills Compared

Profits £	Company £	Sole Trader £	50:50 Partnership £
10,000	737	380	260
20,000	3,317	1,280	760
30,000	5,897	2,180	1,660
40,000	8,724	3,080	2,560
50,000	10,304	3,453	3,460
60,000	11,884	3,653	4,360
70,000	13,464	3,853	5,260
80,000	15,044	4,053	6,160
90,000	16,624	4,253	6,706
100,000	18,204	4,453	6,906
110,000	19,784	4,653	7,106
120,000	21,364	4,853	7,306
130,000	22,944	5,053	7,506
140,000	24,524	5,253	7,706
150,000	26,104	5,453	7,906
160,000	27,684	5,653	8,106
180,000	30,844	6,053	8,506
200,000	34,004	6,453	8,906

Fortunately there are alternative ways for company owners to pay themselves. We'll take a closer look at the most important one in the next chapter.

You may be wondering why the national insurance bill for the partnership is often much higher than that of the sole trader.

If the partnership earns profits of £80,000 each of the two partners will receive £40,000 and pay full national insurance on his share. Profits that would have been subject to just 2% national insurance in the hands of a sole trader, end up being taxed at 9% when the income is split.

In Table 2 we can see that a sole trader earning £40,000 pays £3,080 in national insurance. So the combined bill for a partnership with £80,000 is £6,160 (2 x £3,080).

Chapter 9

Using Dividends to Escape Tax

One way of avoiding a large national insurance bill is to pay yourself a dividend.

Dividends reward your entrepreneurship, not your work for the company, and are therefore not subject to national insurance. National insurance is a tax on 'work' income (salaries, bonuses etc) but not on investment income.

In fact, as we'll see later, dividends can also be used to reduce your income tax.

The important thing to note is that dividends are paid out of profits. If your company doesn't have any profits, it cannot pay any dividends. Also, dividends are paid out of after-tax profits and are not a tax-deductible expense for the business. Salaries and bonuses, on the other hand, are tax-deductible expenses.

Remember, as a company owner, you are concerned about both your tax bill *and* the company's tax bill. So the fact that the company can claim salaries as a tax deduction, but not dividends, is something that has to be borne in mind when you structure your pay. We'll return to this later.

First of all let's examine how dividends are taxed.

9.1 HOW DIVIDENDS ARE TAXED

The tax treatment of dividends can be extremely confusing because of terms like 'tax credit', 'net dividend' and 'gross dividend'. However, as a general rule:

Basic-rate taxpayers pay no tax on dividends.

Higher-rate taxpayers pay 25% tax on dividends.

Additional rate taxpayers pay 36.1% tax on dividends.

If you are interested in the technical details, the taxman treats UK share dividends as having been paid net of tax at 10%. To calculate the gross taxable dividend, a tax credit is added to the cash dividend (by cash dividend I mean the actual money you receive from the company – also known as the net dividend).

This tax credit is calculated by multiplying the cash dividend by the fraction 1/9.

The gross dividend is then taxed at either 10% (if the shareholder is a basic-rate taxpayer), 32.5% (if the shareholder is a higher-rate taxpayer) or 42.5% if your income is over £150,000 and you are taxed at the additional rate.

The tax credit is then deducted from the tax payable, although this can never create a repayment of tax.

This is best illustrated with some examples.

Example 1

Bob owns a company (Bob Limited) and receives a dividend of £25,000 and no other income. Bob's tax bill for the 2011/12 tax year is calculated as follows:

Bob's tax bill on £25,000 dividend:

	£
Cash dividend	25,000
Tax credit @ 1/9	2,778
Gross dividend	27,778
Less: Personal allowance	7,475
Taxable income	20,303
Tax:	
£20,303 @ 10%	2,030
Less: tax credit (restricted)	2,030
Total tax bill	**NIL**

Example 2

If Bob received a £60,000 dividend his tax bill would be:

	£
Cash dividend	60,000
Tax credit @ 1/9	6,667
Gross dividend	66,667
Less: Personal allowance	7,475
Taxable income	59,192
Tax:	
£35,000 @ 10%	3,500
£24,192 @ 32.5%	7,862
Less: tax credit (restricted)	5,919
Total tax bill	**5,443**

Note that if gross dividends are reduced by the personal allowance the tax credit is also reduced. The tax credit is restricted to 10% of £59,192 (total gross dividends less the £7,475 personal allowance).

Example 3

If Bob received a dividend of £200,000 his tax bill would be:

	£
Cash dividend	200,000
Tax credit @ 1/9	22,222
Gross dividend	222,222
Less: Personal allowance	0
Taxable income	222,222
Tax:	
£35,000 @ 10%	3,500
£115,000 @ 32.5%	37,375
£72,222 @ 42.5%	30,694
Less: tax credit	22,222
Total tax bill	**49,347**

9.2   DIVIDENDS VERSUS SALARY

A critical question is, how much better off is Bob by taking dividends instead of salary?

With salaries there is both income tax and national insurance and national insurance is paid by both Bob and his company. If Bob takes a salary of £60,000, his income tax bill for the 2011/12 tax year will be:

	£
Salary	60,000
Less: personal allowance	7,475
Taxable income	52,525
Tax:	
£35,000 @ 20%	7,000
£17,525 @ 40%	7,010

Total income tax   14,010

His tax bill when he took a dividend was only £5,443 compared with £14,010 from taking a salary – a total saving of £8,567.

What about national insurance? Dividends are not subject to national insurance, salary payments are. Both Bob and his company pay national insurance. On a salary of £60,000 national insurance would be payable as follows:

Class 1 primary (paid by Bob)

	£
£42,475 - £7,225 x 12%	4,230
£17,525 x 2%	350
Total	4,580.5

Class 1 secondary (paid by Bob Limited)

£60,000 - £7,072 x 13.8%   7,304.06

By taking a dividend, Bob's total tax bill is £5,443. By taking a salary the total tax and national insurance bill is £25,894.56.

By taking a dividend, Bob has saved £20,451.56 in taxes.

However, before getting too excited it's important to note that we have overlooked one important factor.

As we've stated all along, it's important to look at the tax position of both the owner of the company and the company itself.

Companies cannot claim a tax deduction for dividend payments, whereas salary payments can be claimed. Furthermore, the class 1 secondary national insurance paid by the company is also tax deductible.

The more deductions a company can claim, the lower its corporation tax bill.

Impact on the Company's Tax Bill

So taking a dividend may have decreased Bob's personal tax liability dramatically but it will have increased the company's tax bill.

The critical question is whether the increase in the company's tax bill is offset by the drop in Bob's tax bill.

This important issue will be examined shortly. Clearly there are a lot of interrelating factors that have to be taken into account.

Before we bring it all together in Chapter 10, let's take a look at some of the other practical factors that may influence the dividend/salary decision.

9.3   OTHER IMPORTANT FACTORS

A number of points must be made about dividends:

Minimum Wage Regulations

One factor worth bearing in mind is the national minimum wage. If it applied it would not be possible to extract profits solely by way of dividend. Why? Because as an employee of your company you would need to pay yourself a minimum salary.

In practice, this should not be an issue for most directors because the minimum wage regulations make a distinction between office holders and employees.

Under UK law, company directors are classed as office holders, rather than employees.

Because the minimum wage regulations do not apply to office holders (unless they also have contracts that make them employees), most directors will be exempt from these regulations.

Therefore, in principle, a director could extract cash from a company solely in the form of dividends. However, in practice most directors take a small salary as well.

It is usually beneficial to pay yourself enough salary to make full use of the national insurance threshold. A salary of, say, £7,000 would be free of income tax and national insurance. If your spouse works for the company, your family could receive salary income of £14,000 and pay absolutely no income tax or national insurance.

Furthermore, your company will be able to claim the amounts as a tax deduction. If you decided not to pay the salary, and extracted the cash as dividends instead, the company would lose the £14,000 tax deduction.

Pension Contributions

Pension plans offer several tax benefits that you could lose if you take too much income as dividends. These tax benefits include income tax relief on contributions and tax-free investment growth.

Most people can contribute up to £50,000 into a pension plan every year, provided they have earnings of at least £50,000. The problem with dividends is they do not count as earnings. Salaries do.

If all of your income comes from dividends the maximum pension contribution you can make personally is £3,600 per year (the rules state that everyone under age 75 can make a contribution of £3,600 per year).

This is the *gross* contribution and includes the taxman's repayment of your basic-rate income tax. The maximum cash contribution you can make is £2,880.

One solution for company owners is to get the company to make pension contributions on their behalf. These are certainly very tax efficient, as they generally provide corporation tax relief for the company and also avoid national insurance.

It is possible that HM Revenue & Customs will deny tax relief if the pension contribution, together with the director/shareholder's other remuneration, amounts to more than a commercial rate of pay for the job they do for the company.

This problem is fairly rare in practice but could affect any company owner who does not play a fully active role in the day to day management of their business.

Personal Service Companies

Certain rules known as IR35 apply to personal service companies. The effect of these rules is that the company is deemed to pay an amount of salary on 5th April each tax year. The amount of the deemed payment is calculated by the use of a prescribed formula. This negates any benefit from extracting funds via a dividend.

The aim of the IR35 rules is to eliminate the avoidance of tax and national insurance by setting up a company in circumstances where the individual would otherwise be regarded as an employee of the client.

Prior to the introduction of the legislation, an individual could avoid being taxed as an employee by providing those services through a company. Money could be taken out of the company in the form of dividends instead of salary, thus enjoying a number of tax benefits. HMRC is currently looking at reforming the IR35 rules.

Managed Service Companies

Under rules that apply from 6th April 2007, the taxman is getting tougher with 'Managed Service Companies'.

These are intermediary companies set up to sidestep the IR35 provisions and allow employees to receive dividends instead of salary.

In return for a fee or commission, these intermediary companies take on a number of workers who are both employees and shareholders of the company but with each one holding a different class of share. This allowed the managed service company to pay each of the workers a low salary to utilize the personal allowance, with the remainder of the profits extracted in the form of dividends.

The tax savings were huge not least because national insurance was being avoided in full. The Revenue has been looking closely at individuals artificially using companies to extract salary as dividends, so this was always going to be an area where they would clamp down.

The new provisions will introduce rules similar to those that apply to personal service companies – payments from the company will be deemed to be salary instead of dividends.

Chapter 10

Detailed Examples of Tax Savings

In the previous chapters we have compared corporation tax with income tax, company national insurance with self-employment national insurance and the tax treatment of salaries with dividends.

Now the time has come to throw all of these taxes into the pot and illustrate, with the use of several examples, how much better off you could be by using a company.

The potential tax benefits of using a company depend on many factors including:

- How much profit the company makes

- How much profit you want to reinvest

- The amount of salary you require

- Whether a dividend will be paid

- Whether your spouse or other family members are involved in the business

- How much other taxable income you receive

The examples do not take ALL factors into consideration – that would be impossible.

For example, we ignore the potential loss of tax relief on pension contributions and we ignore any other income the taxpayer may receive, for example income from investments or rental properties.

For this reason you should always speak to your accountant or tax adviser before setting up a company.

Having said that, the examples in this chapter are detailed enough to provide some extremely important insights.

How Much Salary?

In all of the examples in this chapter we assume that the company owner takes a small salary of £7,000. This income will be free of both income tax and national insurance (both employee's and employer's national insurance).

Many company owners take a small salary like this, instead of taking all of their income as dividends. Why? Because companies can claim tax relief on salary payments but not on dividends (dividends are paid out of *after-tax* profits).

By taking a small salary the company owner could end up winning on two counts:

- The company owner receives a totally tax-free salary, and
- The company obtains a tax deduction for the salary

Another reason why it is usually essential to take some salary is to preserve your state pension entitlement.

If you earn less than the 'lower earnings limit' (LEL) during any tax year, that year will not be included in your contribution record when your basic state pension is calculated. For the 2011/12 tax year the LEL is £5,304, so it is essential to pay yourself a salary of at least this amount to protect your contribution record.

We use a £7,000 salary in all of the examples because it is a nice round number and because a salary of this amount makes it easy for the reader to follow the tax calculations – there is no national insurance to worry about and often no income tax.

Employer's national insurance only kicks in when your salary exceeds £7,072, employee's national insurance kicks in when your salary exceeds £7,225 and income tax usually kicks in when your income exceeds £7,475. A salary of £7,000 could escape all three taxes.

Although using a salary of £7,000 is ideal for the purposes of this guide – to give the small business owner some idea of the tax savings to be had by setting up a company – it is not necessarily the *optimal* salary for every company owner.

The optimal salary will often depend on how much profit the company makes. For small companies, with annual profits not exceeding £300,000, it will usually make sense to pay yourself a salary equal to the employee's national insurance earnings threshold (£7,225 for 2011/12), despite the small amount of employer's national insurance payable.

For directors of medium and large companies with profits exceeding £300,000, it will generally be worth paying a salary equal to the personal allowance of £7,475 in 2011/12.

However, whether we use a salary of £7,000 or £7,475 will probably not make a huge amount of difference to the average business owner trying to decide whether or not to start a company.

The best way to see how all of the various taxes interact and see how much money you could possibly save by using a company is to look at some examples.

Example 1

Sharon's sole trader business has taxable profits of £17,475 in 2011/12 and she usually extracts all the profits out of the business. Her income tax and national insurance is calculated as follows:

	£
Taxable profits	17,475
Less: personal allowance	7,475
Taxable income	10,000
£10,000 @ 20%	2,000
National insurance	
Class 2 (£2.50 x 52)	130
Class 4 (£17,475 - £7,225 x 9%)	922.50
Tax and national insurance	**3,052.50**

If the business is conducted through a company, the tax position will depend on how Sharon withdraws the profits.

If she pays herself a salary of £17,475 the income tax position will be exactly the same as above. Sharon would have a personal income tax bill of £2,000 and because the salary is tax deductible, the company will have no taxable profits and therefore no corporation tax to pay.

The national insurance would be different, however. Using a company, Sharon would pay class 1 primary contributions of:

$$£17,475 - £7,225 @ 12\% = £1,230$$

Her company would pay class 1 secondary contributions of:

$$£17,475 - £7,072 @ 13.8\% = £1,435.61$$

A tax deduction would be given for the class 1 secondary contributions paid. However, the total national insurance bill using a company and drawing a salary is a lot higher than as a sole trader – she only pays £1,052.50 national insurance as a sole trader.

If Sharon pays herself a salary of £7,000 and takes the rest of her income as dividends the total tax bill (Sharon and the company) will now look like this:

Company's tax position:

	£
Taxable profits (£17,475 - £7,000 salary)	10,475
Corporation tax @ 20%	2,095
After-tax profits	8,380

Sharon's tax position:

	£
Salary	7,000
Less: Personal allowance	7,000
Dividend (after-tax profits)	8,380
Tax credit @ 1/9	931
Gross dividend	9,311
Less: remaining personal allowance	475
Taxable dividend	8,836
Tax @ 10%	884
Less tax credit	-884
Income tax payable	NIL

No national insurance contributions are payable as dividends are exempt from national insurance and the salary is below the national insurance earnings threshold.

The only tax paid is corporation tax of £2,095.

Total tax saving from using a company:

£3,052 (as a sole trader) *less* £2,095 (using a company) = £957

That's not a bad saving when you consider that Sharon's business profits are only £17,475.

Example 2

Rohan's business generates a profit of £60,000. As a sole trader his total income tax and national insurance would be:

Income tax:	**£**
Profits	60,000
Less: Personal allowance	7,475
Taxable income	52,525
£35,000 @ 20%	7,000
£17,525 @ 40%	7,010
Total income tax	14,010

National Insurance:

Class 2 (£2.50 x 52)	130
£42,475 - £7,225 @ 9%	3,172.50
£60,000 - £42,475 @ 2%	350.50
Total tax & NI	**17,663**

Using a company the tax position is as follows:

Company's tax position: £

Taxable profits (£60,000 - £7,000 salary)	53,000
Corporation tax @ 20%	10,600
After-tax profits	42,400

Rohan's tax position:

Salary	7,000
Less: Personal allowance	7,000
Dividend (after-tax profits)	42,400
Tax credit @ 1/9	4,711
Gross dividend	47,111
Less: remaining personal allowance	475
Taxable dividend	46,636
£35,000 @ 10%	3,500
£11,636 @ 32.5%	3,782
Less tax credit	4,664
Income tax payable	2,618

The company and Rohan's combined tax bill is £13,218. Using a company produces a tax saving of around £4,445.

Example 3

Finally, let's take a look at the impact of taking a small salary, with the remaining cash extracted as a dividend when the business owner earns more than £150,000.

Remember high income earners pay tax at the new 50% additional rate and receive no income tax personal allowance.

Ethan's business generates a profit of £200,000 for the 2011/2012 tax year. As a sole trader, his total income tax and national insurance would be as follows:

Income tax:	£
Profits	200,000
Less: Personal allowance	0
Taxable income	200,000
£35,000 @ 20%	7,000
£115,000 @ 40%	46,000
£50,000 @ 50%	25,000
Total income tax	78,000

National Insurance:

Class 2 (£2.50 x 52)	130
£42,475 - £7,225 @ 9%	3,172.50
£200,000 - £42,475 @ 2%	3,150.50
Total tax & NI	**84,453**

Using a company the tax position would be as follows (assuming a salary of £7,000 with the rest of the profits taken as dividends):

	£
Company profit	193,000
Corporation tax @ 20%	38,600
Available for dividend	154,400
Tax credit @ 1/9	17,156
Gross dividend	171,556

Income tax on salary

| £7,000 @ 20% | 1,400 |

Income tax on dividends

£28,000 @ 10%	2,800
£115,000 @ 32.5%	37,375
£28,556 @ 42.5%	12,136
Income tax	52,311
Less: dividend tax credit	17,156
Income tax payable	35,155

| **Total taxes** | **75,155** |

Using a company and extracting all the profits produces a tax and national insurance saving of £9,298.

Table 3 compares the total tax bill at numerous other profit levels for a sole trader, company and partnership taking into account income tax, national insurance, and corporation tax.

TABLE 3
Total Tax Bills Compared

Profits £	Sole Trader £	Partnership £	Company £
10,000	885	260	600
20,000	3,785	1,770	2,600
30,000	6,685	4,670	4,600
40,000	9,585	7,570	6,600
50,000	13,463	10,470	9,218
60,000	17,663	13,370	13,218
70,000	21,863	16,270	17,218
80,000	26,063	19,170	21,218
90,000	30,263	22,726	25,218
100,000	34,463	26,926	29,218
110,000	40,663	31,126	33,218
120,000	45,853	35,326	38,706
130,000	50,053	39,526	44,300
140,000	54,253	43,726	48,300
150,000	58,453	47,926	52,300
160,000	63,653	52,126	56,300
170,000	68,853	56,326	60,489
180,000	74,053	60,526	65,378
190,000	79,253	64,726	70,267
200,000	84,453	68,926	75,155
210,000	89,653	75,126	80,044
220,000	94,853	81,326	84,933
230,000	100,053	87,506	89,822
240,000	105,253	91,706	94,711
250,000	110,453	95,906	99,600
260,000	115,653	100,106	104,489
270,000	120,853	104,306	109,378
280,000	126,053	108,506	114,267
290,000	131,253	112,706	119,156
300,000	136,453	116,906	124,044

Assumptions:
- There are no associated companies.
- As regards the company, a small salary of £7,000 is paid with the remainder of the profits withdrawn by way of dividend paid to the sole shareholder.
- The sole trader has no employees.
- The partnership is a 50:50 partnership.

TABLE 3
Total Tax Bills Compared (contd)

Profits £	Sole Trader £	Partnership £	Company £
310,000	141,653	122,106	129,077
320,000	146,853	127,306	134,445
330,000	152,053	132,506	139,813
340,000	157,253	137,706	145,181
350,000	162,453	142,906	150,549
400,000	188,453	168,906	177,390
450,000	214,453	194,906	204,230
500,000	240,453	220,906	231,070
550,000	266,453	246,906	257,910
600,000	292,453	272,906	284,751
650,000	318,453	298,906	311,591
700,000	344,453	324,906	338,431
750,000	370,453	350,906	365,272
800,000	396,453	376,906	392,112
850,000	422,453	402,906	418,952
900,000	448,453	428,906	445,792
950,000	474,453	454,906	472,633
1,000,000	500,453	480,906	499,473
1,050,000	526,453	506,906	526,313
1,100,000	552,453	532,906	553,153
1,150,000	578,453	558,906	579,994
1,200,000	604,453	584,906	606,834
1,250,000	630,453	610,906	633,674
1,300,000	656,453	636,906	660,515
1,350,000	682,453	662,906	687,355
1,400,000	708,453	688,906	714,195
1,450,000	734,453	714,906	741,035
1,500,000	760,453	740,906	767,876

Taking a sample profit figure from Table 3 – £100,000 – let's examine how the numbers are calculated:

Sole Trader Tax Calculation

Income tax:	£
£100,000 - £7,475	92,525
£35,000 @ 20%	7,000
£57,525 @ 40%	23,010
Total	30,010

National insurance:	
Class 2 (£2.50 x 52)	130
Class 4:	
£42,475 - £7,225 @ 9%	3,172.50
£100,000 - £42,475 @ 2%	1,150.50
Total	4,323.00

Total income tax & national insurance: £34,463

Partnership Tax Calculation

Each partner pays tax on £50,000 of profits.

Income tax:	£
£50,000 - £7,475	42,525
£35,000 @ 20%	7,000
£7,525 @ 40%	3,010
Total	10,010

National insurance:	
Class 2 (£2.50 x 52)	130
Class 4:	
£42,475 - £7,225 @ 9%	3,172.50
£50,000 - £42,475 @ 2%	150.50
Total	3,323.00

Income tax & national insurance per partner: £13,463

Combined tax and national insurance is £26,926

Company Tax Calculation

The director's salary of £7,000 is not subject to income tax or national insurance thanks to the income tax personal allowance and national insurance earnings threshold.

	£
Corporation tax:	
Taxable profits of company:	
£100,000 - £7,000	93,000
Corporation tax £93,000 @ 20%	18,600
Income tax on dividends:	
Amount available for dividend:	
£93,000 - £18,600	74,400
Add tax credit @ 1/9	8,267
Gross dividend	82,667
Less: remaining personal allowance	475
Taxable dividend	82,192
£35,000 @ 10%	3,500
£47,192 @ 32.5%	15,337
Less tax credit	-8,219
Income tax	10,618

Total tax and national insurance   £29,218

Summary

Looking at Table 3 we can see that, compared with being a sole trader, using a company results in a lower overall tax bill until profits rise above approximately £1,050,000.

For example, a business with £80,000 of profits will save £4,845 in tax by using a company. A business with profits of £200,000 will save £9,298.

The reason why the company loses its attractiveness in purely tax terms as profits rise beyond £1 million is because a big chunk of the company's profits is being taxed at 27.5%. This is substantially higher than the 20% rate payable at lower profit levels.

TABLE 4
Total Tax Bills Compared
Partnership vs Two-Director Company

Taxable profits £	Partnership £	Company £
10,000	260	0
20,000	1,770	1,200
30,000	4,670	3,200
40,000	7,570	5,200
50,000	10,470	7,200
60,000	13,370	9,200
70,000	16,270	11,200
80,000	19,170	13,200
90,000	22,726	15,200
100,000	26,926	18,436
110,000	31,126	22,436
120,000	35,326	26,436
130,000	39,526	30,436
140,000	43,726	34,436
150,000	47,926	38,436

When comparing companies and partnerships, a fairer comparison would be to have *two* company directors/shareholders drawing a salary and taking dividends.

This will result in an even lower overall tax bill due to the availability of two personal allowances and two basic-rate tax bands for tax-free dividend payments.

The tax payable, assuming two directors drawing a salary of £7,000 each, with the remaining profits taken as dividends, is summarised in Table 4.

We've also included the partnership tax from Table 3 for comparison.

Clearly the tax savings become quite impressive as the profits of the business increase. When they reach £100,000 the total tax saving is £8,490!

Big Salary vs Dividends

You may be wondering about the effect on the overall tax bill of paying a high salary, as opposed to dividends, when the company's profits are large. We'll examine this in the next two examples.

Although dividends are subject to lower income tax in the hands of the shareholder, salaries can be claimed as a company tax deduction. At profit levels between £300,000 and £1.5 million the salary deduction is worth £2,750 for every £10,000 paid. (The company's marginal tax rate is 27.5%, so every £10,000 paid in salaries escapes £2,750 in corporation tax.)

However, the profits have to be very high before dividends lose their appeal.

Example

Suppose Cedric Ltd is making annual taxable profits of £400,000. Cedric decides to pay himself a salary of £350,000, with the remainder as dividends.

Corporation tax:	£
Taxable profits	400,000
Less: salary	350,000
Less: employer's national insurance	47,324
Profits	2,676
Corporation tax @ 20%	535
After-tax profits	2,141

Income tax:	
Salary	350,000
Income tax on salary	153,000
Employee's national insurance	10,381
Net dividend	2,141
Income tax @ 36.1%	773

Total tax and national insurance: £212,013

This compares with a total tax bill of just £177,390 from Table 3 when most of the income is taken as a dividend. So Cedric is still better off with dividends when his company is making quite substantial profits.

Let's examine the position if Cedric's business is even more successful and earns significantly higher profits. As company profits increase you have to assess which carries the most 'weight': the lower income tax on dividends versus the tax deductibility of the salary plus certain other salary tax benefits.

Example 2

Suppose Cedric's company makes profits of £2 million per year and he decides to pay himself a salary of £1.75 million, with the remainder as dividends.

Corporation tax:	£
Profits	2,000,000
Less: salary	1,750,000
Less: employer's national insurance	240,524
Taxable profits	9,476
Corporation tax @ 20%	1,895
After-tax profits	7,581

Income tax:	
Salary	1,750,000
Income tax on salary	853,000
National insurance	38,381
Net dividend	7,581
Income tax @ 36.1%	2,737

Total tax and national insurance: £1,136,537

The actual amount Cedric receives as 'take-home pay' therefore is £863,463. However, this compares with £968,430 if the income is taken as a dividend.

Therefore the use of a dividend in this case increases take home pay by over £100,000. One of the reasons for this is that the company doesn't have to pay the whopping £278,905 national insurance charge on a dividend.

In practice, as part of a company's year-end tax planning review, the methods of extracting cash in a tax-effective manner should be looked at in detail.

Some of the issues to consider include:

- Maximising pension contributions (pension contributions can be based on salary but not dividends).

- Reducing company's taxable profits to below £300,000 – the point at which the 27.5% corporation tax rate kicks in.

- Ensuring you receive enough dividends to utilise your tax-free basic-rate tax band.

- Ensuring sufficient salary is paid to prevent a loss of any state benefit entitlements.

One reason for paying a salary could be to make larger pension contributions. Dividends are not classed as 'earnings' for pension contribution purposes, so if you pay yourself dividends only, you can only make the minimum pension contribution of £3,600 per tax year.

However, it should not be forgotten that it is possible for company directors to get the company to make pension contributions on their behalf if their earnings are low.

Finally, in the above examples we have made one very important assumption: all of the profits are taken out of the business. But what if a significant percentage is retained to fund future growth of the business?

This is where companies really show their mettle.

Chapter 11

Reinvesting Profits to Make Bigger Tax Savings

Of course, not all shareholders wish to extract all of the available profits from the company every year. In fact this is one of the key advantages of using a company – it lets you decide whether you wish to withdraw the profits or not.

If you choose to leave funds within the business to fund future growth, only corporation tax will be paid on the profits retained within the company. The directors/shareholders won't have to pay any additional income tax.

By contrast, with a sole trader/partnership, the proprietors of the business are taxed on the annual taxable profits irrespective of whether they are retained within the business or taken out as drawings.

Clearly, retaining profits within the company will significantly reduce the overall tax liability.

Table 5 compares the tax liability of a sole trader and 50:50 partnership with a company at different profit levels.

The difference between this table and Table 3 that we looked at earlier is that the shareholder is extracting only 50% of the profits by way of dividend.

The remaining 50% is retained within the company to fund growth of the business and cover the corporation tax liability.

Again, if the company had two shareholders (to give a fairer comparison with a 50:50 partnership) the total tax payable by the company would be even lower!

The total tax bills shown in Table 5 speaks for themselves: when a business is reinvesting and using retained earnings as a source of finance, using a company can produce big tax savings.

Given that most small companies will be seeking to reinvest at least some of their profits, this is where the key tax benefit of using a company arises.

For example, when profits hit £80,000, using a company could save you £9,445 in tax *every year*. The overall tax savings rise to £11,345 when profits reach £100,000.

For Table 5 we assume that the shareholder/employee takes a salary of £7,000, with the remainder as dividends.

The decision to take a salary or bonus can be complex and should be made only after consulting a qualified accountant or tax adviser. The following points should be borne in mind:

- Dividends are taxed at effective rates of 0%, 25% and 36.1%, bonuses and salary are currently taxed at 20%, 40% and 50%.

- Salary payments fall into the PAYE regime, whereas tax on a dividend is paid by 31 January following the end of the tax year (although payments on account may also be required).

- Dividends are not subject to national insurance.

- The company cannot claim a tax deduction for dividend payments.

TABLE 5
Total Tax Bills Compared
50% Profit Reinvested

Profits £	Sole Trader £	Partnership £	Company £
10,000	885	260	600
20,000	3,785	1,770	2,600
30,000	6,685	4,670	4,600
40,000	9,585	7,570	6,600
50,000	13,463	10,470	8,600
60,000	17,663	13,370	10,600
70,000	21,863	16,270	13,368
80,000	26,063	19,170	16,618
90,000	30,263	22,726	19,868
100,000	34,463	26,926	23,118
110,000	40,663	31,126	26,368
120,000	45,853	35,326	29,618
130,000	50,053	39,526	32,868
140,000	54,253	43,726	36,118
150,000	58,453	47,926	39,368
160,000	63,653	52,126	42,618
170,000	68,853	56,326	46,080
180,000	74,053	60,526	50,511
190,000	79,253	64,726	54,942
200,000	84,453	68,926	58,700
210,000	89,653	75,126	61,950
220,000	94,853	81,326	65,200
230,000	100,053	87,506	68,450
240,000	105,253	91,706	71,700
250,000	110,453	95,906	74,950
260,000	115,653	100,106	78,345
270,000	120,853	104,306	82,150
280,000	126,053	108,506	85,956
290,000	131,253	112,706	89,761
300,000	136,453	116,906	93,567

TABLE 5
Total Tax Bills Compared
50% Profits Reinvested (contd)

Profits £	Sole Trader £	Partnership £	Company £
310,000	141,653	122,106	97,597
320,000	146,853	127,306	102,153
330,000	152,053	132,506	106,708
340,000	157,253	137,706	111,264
350,000	162,453	142,906	115,819
400,000	188,453	168,906	138,597
450,000	214,453	194,906	161,375
500,000	240,453	220,906	184,153
550,000	266,453	246,906	206,931
600,000	292,453	272,906	229,708
650,000	318,453	298,906	252,486
700,000	344,453	324,906	275,264
750,000	370,453	350,906	298,042
800,000	396,453	376,906	320,819
850,000	422,453	402,906	343,597
900,000	448,453	428,906	366,375
950,000	474,453	454,906	389,153
1,000,000	500,453	480,906	411,931
1,050,000	526,453	506,906	434,708
1,100,000	552,453	532,906	457,486
1,150,000	578,453	558,906	480,264
1,200,000	604,453	584,906	503,042
1,250,000	630,453	610,906	525,819
1,300,000	656,453	636,906	548,597
1,350,000	682,453	662,906	571,375
1,400,000	708,453	688,906	594,153
1,450,000	734,453	714,906	616,931
1,500,000	760,453	740,906	639,708

TABLE 6
Total Tax Bills Compared:
One versus two Directors/Shareholders
50% Profit Reinvested

Profits £	One Person £	Two Persons £
10,000	600	0
20,000	2,600	1,200
30,000	4,600	3,200
40,000	6,600	5,200
50,000	8,600	7,200
60,000	10,600	9,200
70,000	13,368	11,200
80,000	16,618	13,200
90,000	19,868	15,200
100,000	23,118	17,200
110,000	26,368	19,200
120,000	29,618	21,200
130,000	32,868	23,486
140,000	36,118	26,736
150,000	39,368	29,986

Comparing a one-shareholder company with a partnership is not really a true comparison. Table 6 shows the total tax payable assuming a two-person company with both shareholders extracting 50% of the gross profits by way of a dividend.

As shown in Table 5, a partnership with profits of £150,000 would pay £47,926 in tax, whereas Table 6 shows that a two-person company reinvesting 50% of profits would only pay £29,986 in tax – a total tax saving of £17,940.

This example shows the potential tax savings that can be achieved when you, for example, bring your spouse into the business.

Clearly using a company can provide significant tax savings in the right circumstances.

Chapter 12

Recent Tax Changes

There have been numerous changes to income tax, national insurance and corporation tax rates in recent years. This book is based on the rates for the 2011/12 tax year.

Recently implemented tax changes include:

- A reduction in corporation tax rates – from April 2011.

- An increase in the tax-free personal allowance to £7,475 – from 6th April 2011.

- A reduction in the £37,400 basic-rate tax band to £35,000 – from 6th April 2011. This will increase the amount of income taxed at 40% and offset any saving from the personal allowance increase if you are a high income earner.

- The withdrawal of the income tax personal allowance when income exceeds £100,000 – from 6th April 2010.

- A 50% additional tax rate for anyone earning over £150,000 per year. The additional rate for dividends is 42.5% – from 6th April 2010.

- A 1% increase in national insurance – from April 2011.

- An increase in the capital gains tax rate for higher-rate taxpayers to 28% (from 18%) – from 23rd June 2010.

We'll take a closer look at some of these changes in the pages that follow.

12.1 CORPORATION TAX CHANGES

In the June 2010 emergency Budget the Chancellor of the Exchequer announced that corporation tax rates would be cut from April 2011. The small companies rate would be reduced from 21% to 20% and the main rate would fall from 28% to 27%.

In the March 2011 Budget the Chancellor announced an additional 1% reduction in the main rate to 26% from April 2011.

The main rate will fall by another 1% in 2012, 1% in 2013 and a further 1% in 2014. This means that by 2014 corporation tax rates will be as follows:

Tax Payable by Companies
from 1ˢᵗ April 2014

On the first £300,000 profits	20%
On profits between £300,000 and £1.5m	23.75%
On profits over £1.5m	23%

These reductions in corporation tax rates will probably make using a company even more attractive.

Under the previous Government, the small companies tax rate was due to *increase* from 21% to 22% in 2011. This increase has not only been abolished, it has been reversed. As a result, owners of small companies (profits under £300,000) will pay less corporation tax in future.

The reduction in the main corporation tax rate from 28% to 23% will generate even greater savings for bigger companies. For example, a company with profits of, say, £500,000 will pay £25,000 less corporation tax *every year* from 2014.

12.2   PERSONAL ALLOWANCE & TAX BAND CHANGES

The income tax personal allowance for taxpayers under age 65 has been increased by £1,000 to £7,475 from 6ᵗʰ April 2011.

However, to ensure that the majority of higher-rate taxpayers do not benefit from the increase, the 20% basic-rate tax band has been reduced to £35,000, increasing the amount of income taxed at 40%.

12.3 NATIONAL INSURANCE CHANGES

On 6th April 2011 national insurance rates were increased by 1% and are currently as follows:

- Employees' Class 1   12%
- Employer's Secondary   13.8%
- Self-employed Class 4   9%
- Additional rate   2%

The additional rate applies to all earned income (employed or self-employed) over the upper earnings limit, which is now aligned with the higher-rate income tax threshold (currently £42,475).

The primary threshold, where national insurance kicks in for *employees*, has been increased from £5,715 to £7,225 from 6th April 2011. The secondary threshold, when *employers* have to start paying, has increased to £7,072.

The 1% increase in national insurance rates has made using a company even more attractive than before. This is because unincorporated businesses (i.e. sole traders and partnerships) will not be able to avoid the increased national insurance payable on their profits.

Company owners, on the other hand, can avoid the increase by paying themselves a small salary and taking the rest of their income as dividends.

12.4 USING A COMPANY TO AVOID THE NEW 50% TAX

The new 50% income tax rate applies to all types of earnings. It therefore affects:

- Employees
- Property traders with substantial trading profits
- Property investors with substantial rental income
- Anyone with substantial investment income
- Businesses with substantial trading profits

Many of the people on the above list will be able to choose between trading or holding assets in their own names or using a company.

The overall tax treatment of companies is still very favourable when compared with the tax treatment of individuals.

The small companies corporation tax rate of 20% is very attractive when compared with income tax rates of 40% or 50%.

Sole trader and partnership profits are also subject to national insurance, whereas company profits are not.

Of course, this tax rate comparison assumes that no profits are extracted from the company. If profits are extracted, there would then be a potential income tax charge.

Many business owners, however, reinvest some of their after-tax profits and using a company and paying tax at 20% instead of 52% (50% income tax plus 2% national insurance) could leave you with significantly more after-tax profit to grow your business.

Of course, cash will probably have to be extracted at some point. Fortunately there are a number of options.

For example, the cash could be extracted by way of dividends. If these are within the basic-rate tax band no additional tax will be payable.

Other ways to extract cash include:

- Becoming non-UK resident and extracting cash as a dividend free of UK income tax.

- Becoming non-UK resident and extracting cash as a capital distribution. This would be free of UK capital gains tax, provided the shareholder was non-UK resident for at least five complete tax years.

- Remaining UK resident and extracting cash by way of a capital distribution.

A capital distribution is subject to capital gains tax instead of income tax.

In order to extract cash as capital rather than income the company would need to be wound up. The cash paid out would be treated as share disposal proceeds. The gain would then be taxed at 28% if you are a higher-rate taxpayer (but possibly just 10% if Entrepreneurs Relief is available).

Of course, the profits would have already suffered corporation tax at 20% or more. However, in some cases this would still be less than the income tax and national insurance paid by sole traders and partnerships.

12.5   CAPITAL VS INCOME

In the 2010 emergency Budget the capital gains tax rate payable by higher-rate taxpayers was increased from 18% to 28%. Basic-rate taxpayers still pay 18% tax on their capital gains.

Although this is a significant increase in the CGT rate, capital gains are still taxed much more leniently than income, especially if you qualify for Entrepreneurs Relief.

With Entrepreneurs Relief every individual can have up to £10 million of capital gains from selling a business taxed at just 10%. Every person qualifies, so couples can enjoy up to £20 million taxed at 10%.

The potential tax saving from Entrepreneurs Relief over normal CGT is £1.8 million per person or £3.6 million for couples.

Those who stand to benefit most are 'serial entrepreneurs' — those who build and sell companies or buy and sell companies for a living. This type of business owner could pay tax at just 10%, whereas their fellow business owners, who earn salaries or dividends, could end up paying tax at over 50%.

Trading vs Non-Trading Assets

If you have built up significant cash reserves in a business any disposal or transfer of shares in the company could be 'penalised', as the shares may not qualify for Entrepreneurs Relief. This is because the Entrepreneurs Relief provisions don't count a company as a trading company if it has 'substantial' non-trading assets (such as cash) or income.

Substantial in this context is taken to mean at least 20% of net assets or income. Revenue and Customs will consider any form of non-trading asset for this purpose including rental property, as well as surplus cash not required for the purposes of the trade.

Therefore anyone wanting to maximise the benefit of the company's retained profits may suffer a tax penalty in the future. However, even if Entrepreneurs Relief is not available, the 28% CGT rate is still substantially less than the 50% income tax rate.

Chapter 13

When Using a Company Increases Your Tax

Most of this book is devoted to explaining how you can reduce your tax bill by using a company.

However, this is not always the case. In fact in some cases using a company could end up costing you more in terms of either taxes or other fees.

In this chapter we are therefore going to run through some of the situations where using a company may not be beneficial.

13.1 THE CLOSE INVESTMENT COMPANY (CIC) DANGER

CICs are treated differently to other companies in a couple of important respects. The main difference is that, no matter what their profits are, they are always taxed at the maximum 26% rate of corporation tax.

The tax legislation states that any close company is a CIC unless, throughout the accounting period, it exists wholly or mainly for one or more of the following purposes:

"a) the purpose of carrying on a trade or trades on a commercial basis,
 b) the purpose of making investments in land or estates or interests in land In cases where the land is, or is intended to be, let to persons other than:

> i) *any person connected with the relevant company, or* ~
> ii) *any person who is the wife or husband of an individual connected with the relevant company, or is a relative, or the wife or husband of a relative, of such an individual or of the husband or wife of such an individual..."*

Therefore if you are using a company as a (non-property) investment company the chances are you will be caught by these CIC provisions.

This would include holding intangible assets or investing in shares via a company.

Property investment companies have a specific 'get-out-of-jail' card in the legislation – provided the properties are let to unconnected parties the company will not be a CIC.

If, however, you use a separate property company to hold property that is rented out to your trading company you could easily fall within the scope of the CIC rules.

When the CIC rules apply the company is taxed at 26%, irrespective of the level of profits. When you consider that this is just the *company's* tax charge and that additional tax could be payable by the shareholders/directors when they extract any money from the business, it is quite possible to end up paying more tax using a company than investing personally.

13.2   EMIGRATION PLANNING

This is something that many people overlook, but given the number of people emigrating and working overseas, it's important to bear in mind.

Imagine this. You write a few e-books and decide to sell them over the internet. You know all about the tax benefits of UK companies and decide to transfer the book rights to the company.

Five years later the company is generating royalties of £75,000 per annum. You are fed up living in the UK and want to move to Cyprus.

There is no problem with you personally moving to Cyprus. The problem is that the rights to the books are locked inside the UK company. The company will therefore continue paying UK tax on the book profits.

Any transfer of the books out of the company would result in the company having a taxable capital gain, based on the market value of the books.

There is also a danger that if you stop trading through the company after leaving the country (to prevent further income being taxed in the UK), the taxman could class the company as a CIC, thereby forcing it to pay tax at 26%.

The other downside of retaining a UK company is that you cannot completely sever your ties with the UK, as you will still be in receipt of UK dividends.

You could incorporate an overseas company to hold the shares but this is messy and could lead to an increase in the number of associated companies with all the problems this brings (see Section 6.3).

If you are a sole trader you don't have any of these problems. There is no deemed disposal of assets when you cease to be UK resident (unlike in many countries) and you could just continue running the business from overseas. Provided you have no UK trade there will then be no UK tax payable.

13.3   OCCUPYING PROPERTY

If you are purchasing property that you may occupy personally this should not be owned by a company.

Using a company in these circumstances has a number of disadvantages including:

- If you sell the property you will have to pay corporation tax on the profits and possibly income tax when you extract the proceeds.

- Companies enjoy far fewer reliefs than individuals. In particular individuals who occupy their properties qualify for Principal Private Residence (PPR) Relief, Private Letting Relief and the annual CGT exemption. In many cases these will reduce the tax bill to zero. Companies are not entitled to any of these reliefs and have to pay corporation tax on their gains. The main relief they get is Indexation Relief which protects them from inflation.

- If you occupy a property owned by the company without paying rent at the full market rate, this will be treated as a benefit in kind on which you will have to pay tax.

So owning a residence via a company is clearly a big no-no.

13.4   NON UK DOMICILED

If you claim non-domiciled tax status, you are generally taxed on overseas income and gains to the extent that the income or proceeds are remitted to the UK (i.e., brought into the UK).

In this case, if you own overseas assets or are conducting a trade overseas, using a UK company may not be advisable. A UK company would usually be classed as resident in the UK and as such would be subject to corporation tax on its worldwide income and gains.

13.5   INCORPORATION FOLLOWED BY A QUICK SALE

Transferring your business to a company could be disastrous if you are then made 'an offer you can't refuse' for the shares.

As the owner of the unincorporated business you could probably benefit from Entrepreneurs Relief when you sell and pay capital gains tax at 10% on up to £10 million of gains.

When you transfer the business to a company that you set up, you then own shares instead of business assets and a new period of ownership begins. A disposal of the shares within 12 months of setting up the company would disqualify you from receiving any Entrepreneurs Relief.

Even if you incorporated the company years before and left it dormant you wouldn't have more than one year qualifying ownership, as the company would only become a trading company when the sole trader business is transferred into it.

13.6   IF YOU CAN'T RETAIN PROFITS IN THE COMPANY

The benefit of using a company is that it may have a lower tax rate than you do personally. If you extract cash from the company you then incur a personal tax charge which could eliminate much of the benefit.

So, if you operate as a sole trader or partnership you may suffer a 50% tax charge (as well as national insurance). If you operate via a company, the company may suffer a tax charge of 20% (if the profits are less than £300,000) and you could suffer an effective tax rate of 25% or 36.1% on any dividend payments.

As we've seen in this guide, the big advantage of using a company comes from retaining profits within the company. You then avoid the 50% income tax rate and national insurance.

13.7   OFFSETTING INTEREST

Whilst both companies and individuals are subject to similar rules when it comes to deducting expenses, one aspect that is often overlooked is that sole traders have more flexibility when it comes to structuring their bank accounts.

For example, by using an offset mortgage for your personal residential property you can offset your business bank accounts against your personal mortgage.

This could save you substantial amounts of interest as well as allowing the loan to be repaid much quicker.

For instance, if you have £20,000 in your business bank account you could offset this against your personal mortgage thereby saving you from paying interest at, say, 4%. Effectively this means you will be earning 4% tax free on your business bank account – in other words £800 tax free!

Company owners cannot offset the company's cash against the owner's personal mortgage because they are separate legal entities. Cash has to be held separately in a company bank account.

At the time of writing banks were paying very little interest to companies, often no more than 0.1%. On a balance of £20,000 that would be interest of just £20 per year! This interest would then be taxed leaving you with probably just £16.

So the sole trader in this example would be £784 better off.

When you consider that many businesses carry substantial cash sums (for example retained profits and amounts set aside to pay corporation tax, VAT and PAYE) a sole trader could easily end up saving several thousand pounds per year with an offset mortgage.

13.8 CONCLUSION

The purpose of this chapter is to highlight the fact that there is very rarely a simple strategy that is correct for everyone. For many business owners using a UK company would be advisable – for others, however, it could prove costly.

Make sure you carefully consider the benefits and drawbacks of using a company to carry out your trade or investment activities, as once you have assets locked inside the company, extracting them can be difficult.

Chapter 14

How to Pay Dividends

In many of the examples in the previous chapters the company director/shareholder was paid a very small salary. For cash flow reasons you may need to extract more money than this. If so, the question is: how often can a dividend be paid?

In theory, there is nothing to prevent dividends being paid even weekly. However, such frequent payments could be scrutinised by Revenue and Customs who may argue that the payments are in fact salary and therefore PAYE and national insurance are payable. It is for this reason that directors' loan accounts are often used.

14.1 DIRECTORS LOAN ACCOUNTS

A loan account is used by employees, usually controlling directors, to withdraw cash from the company. A dividend is then paid to clear the loan account, at a given time. This potentially eliminates the need to pay monthly dividends. Instead a dividend can be paid every, say, three months to clear the loan account.

There are a few issues that need to be borne in mind when considering the use of loan accounts:

- A taxable benefit in kind arises if the total balance of all loans outstanding to the director throughout the tax year exceeds £5,000. The benefit in kind is calculated as the difference between the interest actually charged and the interest that should have been levied using Revenue's 'official rate of interest' (currently 4%).

- If the loan is still outstanding nine months and one day after the company's year end, a tax charge equivalent to 25% of the amount of the loan must be paid to Revenue and Customs. This tax charge is repayable if the loan is repaid, however.

- If the loan account is cleared with a salary payment, the taxman will treat the amount of the loan as being subject to PAYE.

Example

Jack and his wife own the entire share capital of their company, Hill Limited. They need to withdraw profits regularly to fund their living expenses but would rather not pay salary, due to the adverse income tax and national insurance implications.

They could certainly pay themselves a small salary with very little tax impact. For example, a salary of £7,000 per year each could be paid with no tax or national insurance cost. The company would then obtain a tax deduction for the £14,000 payment.

They could then withdraw cash as directors up to the £5,000 limit, before clearing this with a dividend payment.

Therefore they could each extract further cash of, say, £1,000 per month for four months, before paying a dividend to clear the remaining balance. If possible, the dividend should actually be paid to the directors, as opposed to, for example, relying on a simple bookkeeping entry to reduce the loan account and reflect a dividend payment.

One key factor to bear in mind here is that in order for a dividend payment to be made, the company must have sufficient distributable profits.

Distributable profits are, broadly speaking, accumulated profits less losses. Therefore if a company has made losses of £100,000 in the period since incorporation, yet makes a profit of £50,000, it does not yet have any distributable profits, as the company is showing an accumulated loss of £50,000.

14.2 HOW TO MAKE A DIVIDEND PAYMENT

It is important when making a payment to employees/directors that it is correctly classed as salary or dividend. This may seem fairly obvious but there are a number of factors that Revenue and Customs will look at to determine whether a payment is in fact salary.

In general terms it is for the directors and shareholders of a company to determine the dividend payments and therefore, provided all proper procedures have been followed, any attempt by the taxman to argue that a payment should be reclassified as salary would be unlikely to be successful.

You could pay a salary equivalent to the employers national insurance threshold of £7,072 if you want to avoid all national insurance. While there is nothing actually wrong with paying such a salary (as this will ensure no income tax or national insurance is payable), many small businesses prefer to pay a round figure, such as £7,000.

The tax anti-avoidance provisions that HMRC has at its disposal are fairly specific and are in the most part cumbersome to apply. Simply paying a salary equivalent to the national insurance threshold would be unlikely to fall foul of these anti-avoidance provisions, provided proper procedures are followed.

The only current risk in paying a non-commercially low salary is that Revenue has used this as one of the factors in assessing whether the 'settlement provisions' should be used against husband and wife companies.

The settlement provisions allow the taxman to argue that, by paying a low salary and the remainder as dividends to two or more shareholders, the dividends should be taxed solely on the main 'working' shareholder.

The Revenue did publish draft 'income shifting' provisions to try and bring some clarity to this area, however these have now been indefinitely suspended. Nevertheless, the payment of an artificially low salary could be taken into account by HMRC.

In addition, in order to obtain a tax deduction for any salary payments, the salary would need to be shown to be made wholly and exclusively for the purposes of the company's trade. The taxman could therefore challenge a salary paid to a non-working spouse who has little input into the running of the business.

It is therefore sensible to keep records of the work undertaken in exchange for the salary payments or other evidence showing the cost of obtaining similar services from a third party.

There are a number of formalities that should be observed when making dividend and salary payments to ensure that the correct legal procedures are followed.

The question of whether a dividend is unlawful or not is determined by the company's articles of association and the Companies Act and is not primarily an issue for HMRC.

The articles are essentially the internal rules of the company and will determine how the company is run. It is possible to have customized articles drafted by a lawyer but, in most cases, the company formation agent will simply use a standard template.

It would be the responsibility of the directors or company secretary to consider the legality of dividend payments.

If the correct procedures are not followed, the taxman could argue that a dividend payment has not been lawfully made. They could then class the payments as salary, and subject them to PAYE and national insurance or, more likely, illegal dividends could be classed as a loan to directors, with the possibility of both a company and personal tax charge.

Generally the shareholders must agree to any dividend payment, although for interim dividends (payments during the accounting period) the directors may authorise payment, without shareholders consent at a general meeting.

In most cases this will not be a big issue if the shareholders are also the directors. The following formalities should be observed when making dividend payments:

- Minutes of directors' meetings authorising the dividend should be drafted and dated.

- Dividend vouchers showing the net and gross dividend paid per share, along with the total amount paid should be issued by the company secretary to the shareholders.

- You should retain evidence (forecasts etc) to support your view that there are sufficient distributable profits to make a dividend payment. If there is any doubt as to whether there will be sufficient distributable profits you should draw up interim accounts to determine the level of distributable profits.

- The dividend payments should be correctly recorded in the company's accounting records.

14.3 ILLEGAL DIVIDENDS

There is a big difference between the treatment of legal and illegal dividends. Legal dividends are dividends that are made out of company profits with the correct payment procedures being followed.

Illegal dividends would usually be made where the company does not have sufficient retained profits to cover the dividend payments. In this case, the excess would be classed as illegal. That is why it is important to ensure that the company has enough profits (note profits, not cash). If there is any doubt, draft accounts should be drawn up.

The Companies Act states that a shareholder who knows or has reasonable grounds to believe that a dividend or part of it is unlawful is liable to repay it or that part of it to the company.

There is an exception if the shareholder is innocent and doesn't know the dividend is illegal, although this will only really apply to larger quoted companies. In most small private companies, particularly where the directors are also the controlling shareholders, the taxman would assume that the shareholders know the status of the dividend.

Where this applies the company is not classed as distributing income to the shareholder, and the shareholder holds the cash as a trustee for the company. In essence for most small private companies, this will mean that it will be treated as a loan to the shareholder with the associated tax implications.

This is potentially costly in tax terms, as the company could be landed with a 25 per cent tax charge on the amount of the loan and the shareholder/director could be taxed on the benefit in kind at a market interest rate.

Chapter 15

Using Your Spouse for Further Tax Savings

Company owners are often advised to make full use of their spouse's tax-free personal allowances and basic-rate tax bands.

Remember you pay no tax on your dividends if your income falls into the basic-rate tax band. There are two decisions to make:

- Whether to employ your spouse and pay him or her a salary, with the company claiming this payment as a tax deduction.

- Whether your spouse should subscribe for shares in the company on incorporation and receive dividends.

These are important decisions because there are significant tax savings to be had if you get it right.

In Table 7 we compare the taxes of a one-person company with a two-person company based on a salary of £7,000 per person. The one-person company has only one shareholder/director so use is made of only one tax-free personal allowance and one basic-rate tax band. The two-person company has two directors and two shareholders so it's possible to make use of an extra tax-free personal allowance and an extra basic-rate tax band.

There's a big difference between the tax bills, no matter how much profit the company is making. For example, even if the company is only making profits of £20,000, the tax bill falls £1,400. The tax savings increase as the profits go up until, when profits hit £130,000, the maximum tax saving of £13,864 is achieved.

This is all very well but you may have to be careful about bringing your spouse into the business. A few years ago Revenue and Customs became increasingly interested in husband and wife companies and in some cases challenged techniques similar to those outlined above and demanded significant tax payments (sometimes up to £50,000 in back taxes).

TABLE 7
Total Tax Bills Compared:
One versus two Directors/Shareholders

Profits £	One Person £	Two Persons £
10,000	600	0
20,000	2,600	1,200
30,000	4,600	3,200
40,000	6,600	5,200
50,000	9,218	7,200
60,000	13,218	9,200
70,000	17,218	11,200
80,000	21,218	13,200
90,000	25,218	15,200
100,000	29,218	18,436
110,000	33,218	22,436
120,000	38,706	26,436
130,000	44,300	30,436
140,000	48,300	34,436
150,000	52,300	38,436

15.1 WHAT IS THE TAXMAN'S THINKING?

Revenue and Customs took a dislike to small business owners artificially splitting their profits with their spouses a few years ago.

They originally challenged this practice by using the 'settlements legislation' to challenge the income paid to non-working spouses.

The settlement provisions provide that where a person makes a settlement (essentially a gift) any income that arises will be taxed in the hands of the person who made the gift.

This potentially creates a problem for married couples who want to shift business income from a spouse with a high tax rate to a spouse with a low tax rate.

Revenue and Customs applied the settlements legislation very widely although, as it relates to husband and wife companies, two key situations were being targeted:

- Husband and wife companies where both subscribed for shares when the company was formed.

- Husband and wife companies where one spouse subscribes for shares when the company is set up and subsequently gifts some of the shares to the other spouse.

Both of these scenarios are very common and the effect of the settlements legislation applying would be that dividends received by the basic-rate taxpayer are assessed on the other spouse, frequently a higher-rate taxpayer.

This would then effectively eliminate the benefit of having a second shareholder. Looking at Table 7, a company with profits of £100,000 could see an increase of £10,782 in its tax bill.

If Revenue and Customs were to look back for up to six years (as they can) there could be a hefty additional tax charge due.

In both of the above situations the taxman has looked for companies which have a low capital base, with the majority of the work undertaken by just one of the spouses.

The low capital value of the company indicates to the taxman that the shares do not represent ownership rights over a large amount of assets but are, in effect, simply a right to income from the company.

However, although Revenue & Customs was convinced it was right and the settlements provisions could apply to dividends received in these situations, senior judges did not agree.

The infamous 'Arctic Systems' case went right the way to the House of Lords before it was decided that the settlement provisions did not apply.

Therefore in most cases the Revenue would now find it difficult to apply the settlements provisions successfully to dividend extractions from small husband and wife companies and shareholders can submit current tax returns on the basis that they are each taxed on the receipts.

This means that both you and your spouse would complete tax returns with dividend income being split to take advantage of the two basic-rate tax bands. You would not need to complete details of any settlement on the trust pages of the tax return.

15.2   NEW LEGISLATION ON THE HORIZON?

This may not however be the end of the matter.

Revenue & Customs was determined to address the issue of small husband and wife companies artificially using the two basic rate tax bands and planned to introduce legislation to apply from 6 April 2008.

This is known as the 'income shifting' legislation and seeks to achieve the same result as using the settlement provisions.

To start off the Government announced that the 'income shifting' legislation was put on hold until April 2009 to allow further consultation.

Then in the 2008 Pre-Budget Report it was announced that plans to introduce the income shifting legislation have been put on ice for now.

This was a welcome announcement as it continues to allow small companies flexibility in the way they pay director/shareholders.

It's worth bearing in mind, however, that although the income shifting legislation has been put on hold, the Government may well introduce provisions to counteract the tax benefits of dividends paid to a non-working spouse at some point in the future.

As establishing a company is a long term tax planning strategy, you should therefore bear in mind that, although you may be able to make full use of your spouse's basic rate tax band and personal allowance at the moment, this may not necessarily be the case in the future.

15.3 JOINT ASSETS

One of the little-known changes made in the 2004 Budget was to change the income tax treatment of certain jointly held assets.

Previously, income from assets such as shares jointly held by a husband and wife was automatically taxed 50:50, irrespective of the actual beneficial ownership of the shares. One spouse was allowed to own the majority of the shares but income tax savings were achieved by dividing the dividends equally. If required, an election was allowed to be made to have income taxed according to the actual beneficial entitlements.

This loophole was being used to circumvent the settlement provisions.

Under the 2004 rules, the 50:50 basis will no longer apply, and the dividends from shares in close companies (which will in practice include practically all small owner-managed companies) will be taxed according to the actual ownership interests.

15.4 SUMMARY

Husband and wife companies are in a relatively good position at the moment. The current position is that the settlements provisions do not apply and they can therefore generally each make use of their basic rate tax band.

The decision in the 2008 Pre-Budget Report to suspend the implementation of the new income shifting rules is welcome as in practice applying these rules would be very difficult.

Therefore whilst the current tax year provides further opportunities for small companies to reduce tax by using dividends, this is an area that should be carefully monitored. If new anti-avoidance rules do get implemented it may then be worthwhile considering a transfer of shares or payment of a market rate salary to establish an arm's length basis for any remuneration. If any provisions are introduced in the future they are likely to have an exemption for arm's length transactions.

Finally, remember that the tax treatment of husband and wife companies is complex. Always seek professional advice on how to structure your pay.

15.5   DIVIDEND WAIVERS

We are sometimes asked whether all shareholders need to receive a dividend, or whether you can 'pick and choose' who receives payment. Clearly such flexibility would be advantageous, as you would be able to channel profits to the shareholder with the lowest income in any particular tax year.

However, this is not the case. Dividends are payable in direct proportion to your shareholding. Therefore a 33% shareholder would in general be entitled to 33% of the declared dividend.

There are, however, other options available. Firstly, different classes of share capital could be used, for example A and B shares. The dividend declared for A shares could be different to the B shares, or alternatively preference shares could be used, giving the shareholder a fixed income return on their investment, yet allowing this to be still taxed as a dividend receipt.

Revenue and Customs can and has applied the settlements legislation to preference shares used to split income, as arguably they represent little more than a right to income. (At least with ordinary shares there is the argument that the shares represent a lot more than just the right to receive dividends because the shares ultimately relate to the underlying assets of the company.)

Secondly, a shareholder could waive the right to receive dividends. The risk here is that Revenue and Customs could apply either the settlement provisions or the income shifting rules (if implemented).

The taxman can argue that the person making the waiver has indirectly provided funds to another and that the settlements legislation should be used.

Much would depend on the facts of the dividend waiver, however the taxman would be on the look out for the following factors, which would indicate that the settlements legislation is likely to apply:

- The level of retained profits is not enough to allow the same rate of dividend to be paid to all shareholders.

- Although there are sufficient retained profits to pay the same rate of dividend per share for the year in question, there has been a history of waivers over several years where the total dividends payable in the absence of the waivers exceed profits.

- Evidence suggesting that the same rate would not have been paid to all shareholders in the absence of the waiver.

- The non-waiving shareholders are persons whom the waiving shareholder can reasonably be regarded as wishing to benefit by the waiver.

- The non-waiving shareholder would pay less tax on the dividend than the waiving shareholder.

The income shifting rules could apply (if they are implemented) if one shareholder has foregone income that he was entitled to and would have been reasonably expected to have received given his input into the company.

Therefore if there is any hint of the dividend waiver being used to reduce tax by transferring income to a fellow shareholder and the arrangement is not on an arm's length basis, such waivers may need to be reconsidered in the future.

In addition, a dividend waiver could be a potentially exempt transfer (PET) for inheritance tax purposes and, as such, the amount of the waiver would be classed as part of the giftor's estate unless they survived for at least seven years from the date of the gift.

If you're contemplating a dividend waiver you need to carefully consider whether it could be questioned by Revenue and Customs. In particular, it is essential that there are sufficient profits to distribute the chosen dividend to all shareholders if desired.

15.6 RETAINING CASH WITHIN THE COMPANY

One point that is sometimes raised is whether cash can be retained within the company and subsequently extracted a number of years later. This may be due to cash-flow issues or potential offshore tax planning opportunities (see Chapter 19).

In general there will be few significant issues with this strategy. If money was left on loan account, the company could be charged interest by the shareholder (at a market rate). This would be allowed as a tax-deductible expense for the company and would be taxed as interest income in the shareholder's hands.

This would be taxed before dividends and could potentially have the effect of pushing more of the dividends into the higher-rate tax band. The cash retained in the company would already have suffered a corporation tax charge. The only impact would be if the cash balances were significant.

In order to qualify as a business asset for both capital gains tax and inheritance tax, and thereby benefit from Entrepreneurs Relief and Business Property Relief, the company must be a trading company.

When assessing whether a company is a trading company, Revenue and Customs will look at a variety of issues, including the annual accounts.

The taxman has stated that if there are significant non-trading assets, this could impair the trading status of the company, with the result that Entrepreneurs Relief and Business Property Relief could be restricted.

One of the examples they have traditionally given of non-trading assets would be substantial cash retained in the company, and not required for a trading purpose. This is to prevent 'money box' companies from obtaining enhanced tax reliefs.

What is 'significant' in this context is generally regarded as being either 20% of net assets, or 20% of income.

If the cash was retained for a trading purpose there would be no problem. However it would not otherwise be advisable to build up large cash balances within the company that could be regarded as an 'investment activity'.

15.7   HOW MANY SHARES SHOULD BE ISSUED?

This is entirely a matter for you as the prospective shareholders and directors of the company. In general I would advise that a share capital of at least £100 is retained. This will then allow for easier distribution of shares.

One common situation would be for directors/shareholders to wish to reduce the size of their estates for inheritance tax reasons. If share capital of only £2 was issued this would be more complex than if £100 of share capital was originally subscribed for. The shareholders could then transfer five or 10 shares to family members (hopefully claiming full capital gains tax and inheritance tax relief).

Chapter 16

Incorporating an Existing Business

In this chapter we explore the tax consequences of incorporating an existing sole trader business. Naturally this is more complicated than trading through a company from day one.

As you will see there are lots of issues to consider and traps to avoid. Make sure you speak to your accountant before you act.

16.1 INCOME TAX AND CAPITAL ALLOWANCES

The transfer of an unincorporated business to a company results in a 'cessation of trade'. Choosing the correct day on which to cease trading can provide you with a significant opportunity to defer your final income tax payments.

By delaying the incorporation by two or three months, in certain circumstances it is possible to defer paying the final tax bill for the unincorporated business by up to 12 months.

A cessation of trade also normally results in 'balancing adjustments' to capital allowances.

It is important to understand that the purpose of the capital allowances legislation is to provide tax relief for the total cost of an asset *over its lifetime*. Therefore suppose that an asset is acquired for £10,000 and after three years, tax relief of £5,000 has been obtained through the capital allowance system. If in year four the asset is sold for £8,000, there would normally be a balancing charge of £3,000.

The 'loss' to the business was effectively £2,000 because the asset was bought for £10,000 and sold for £8,000. As tax relief of £5,000 has been given, the additional £3,000 is clawed back. This amount would then be 'added back' in calculating profits.

However, if the disposal of the assets of the business is to a company controlled by the sole trader or partners, a form of relief is available to avoid these balancing charges.

It is possible for the business to transfer the plant and machinery to the company at its open market value and for the potential balancing charge to be avoided by making a joint election under the 'succession' provisions contained in the capital allowances legislation.

The effect of the election is to treat the business as transferring the plant and machinery to the company at a price which produces no balancing allowance/charge (in other words, at the tax written-down value at which the business holds the assets).

The new company's capital allowances are calculated as though it had always owned the transferred plant and machinery. There is therefore a continuity of capital allowances, with no balancing adjustments.

16.2 CAPITAL GAINS TAX (CGT)

Often the key consideration when disposing of a business is the amount of capital gains tax payable. The good news is that CGT can usually be avoided completely when you incorporate an existing sole trader business or partnership.

The disposal of an unincorporated business is treated for taxation purposes as a disposal of the assets employed in the business. It will, therefore, be necessary to prepare computations of the chargeable gains and allowable losses in respect of all chargeable assets including:

- Goodwill
- Land and buildings
- Fixed plant and machinery
- Tangible moveable property with a market value in excess of £6,000 (usually applies to large pieces of plant and machinery).

How the Gain is Calculated

A typical capital gains tax calculation looks like this:

Proceeds (1)	X
Less: Incidental costs of disposal (2)	(X)
Less: Acquisition cost (3)	(X)
Less: Incidental costs of acquisition	(X)
Less: Enhancement expenditure (4)	(X)
Less: Reliefs	(X)
Less: Annual exemption	(X)
Chargeable gain	**X**

Notes:

(1) The disposal proceeds will, in the majority of cases, be the market value of the assets at the date of incorporation.

(2) Incidental costs of disposal/acquisition include legal fees relating to the disposal/purchase, stamp duty, auctioneer's fees etc.

(3) The cost of the asset is the original cost of the asset. There are special rules for assets acquired before 31 March 1982 and 5 April 1965.

(4) Enhancement expenditure is expenditure incurred in improving the value of the asset that has not obtained tax relief in another form. It must also be reflected in the state and nature of the asset at the date of disposal.

So, for example, expenditure incurred in refurbishing and extending a restaurant property prior to sale would be likely to qualify as enhancement expenditure.

In the case of a rapidly expanding business, the value of the goodwill may be substantial. Similarly, land and property that has been owned for a significant period could also generate large gains.

Reliefs

There are two main methods of avoiding a capital gains tax charge when you incorporate a business. These are:

- Incorporation Relief
- Gift Relief

Incorporation Relief provides for a form of 'rollover' relief if ALL the assets of the business are transferred as a going concern to the company in exchange for shares issued by the company.

Gift Relief provides for a form of 'holdover' relief where individuals transfer business assets to the company for a consideration which is less than the market value of the assets. Both of these reliefs are mutually exclusive.

We shall look at these two methods in further detail below, as it is important to fully assess the capital gains tax position when you incorporate.

Incorporation Relief

The capital gains tax liability on the incorporation of a business can be deferred in whole or in part provided that:

- All the assets of the business (excluding cash if desired) are transferred to the company, and

- The business is transferred as a going concern, and

- The business is transferred wholly or partly in exchange for shares issued by the company to the person(s) transferring the business.

It is Revenue's view that most commercial businesses will qualify for this relief, although they have stated that they would resist granting this relief on the transfer of a 'passive' holding of investments or an investment property. This reinforces the point made at the beginning of the guide that certain reliefs are given only to *trading* businesses.

Example

Ethan commenced trading in May 1987 as a builder's merchant. His business has been successful and he now wishes to incorporate by forming BM Ltd. A summary of the assets of the business, including current market values, is as follows:

	Market value £'000	Book value £'000	Cost £'000
Land & buildings	500	150	150
Plant & equipment (each item valued at less than £6,000)	50	50	125
Goodwill	200	-	-
Stock	100	100	-
Cash	60	60	-
Less: Trade creditors	-150	-150	-
Total	760	210	275

If Ethan incorporates his business wholly in exchange for shares, the following chargeable gains will arise:

Land & buildings	**£'000**
Market value	500
Cost	-150
Indexation	-90
Gain	260

Goodwill	
Market value	200
Cost	-
Indexation	-
Gain	200

Total chargeable gains: £260,000 + £200,000 = £460,000.

As BM Ltd will take over all the assets (except cash) and liabilities, shares will be issued with a CGT base cost of:

$$£760,000 - £60,000 = £700,000$$

The effect of the Incorporation Relief is to reduce the base cost of the shares by the amount of the chargeable gains to be rolled over. In this case the revised base cost of the shares would be:

$$£700,000 - £460,000 = £240,000$$

This would have the effect of rolling over the gain arising on incorporation until the shares in the company are disposed of. If there are assets owned by the business that are not used for trading purposes, for example investments or land that is surplus to business requirements and rented out to tenants, it would be necessary to not transfer such assets to the company as any chargeable gains arising on the transfer would be unlikely to qualify for the relief. However, this should be confirmed with the local Inspector of Taxes as, if not accepted, it could lead to you losing any claim to Incorporation Relief.

It should be noted that if the chargeable gain on incorporation exceeds the cost of the shares issued to the owners of the unincorporated business, the excess gain is subject to capital gains tax as normal and Incorporation Relief would not be available.

The disadvantage of Incorporation Relief is that ALL of the assets of the business must be transferred to the company. This is likely to be expensive in terms of stamp duty land tax if there are any business premises. However, if assets are retained in order to save stamp duty a capital gains tax charge may then arise on all the chargeable assets transferred to the company.

Another condition for Incorporation Relief is that the business must be transferred in exchange for shares issued by the company to the person transferring the business. If the shares were therefore issued to the son of the person disposing of the business, this would restrict the availability of relief as the son would not be a proprietor of the sole trader business.

If the father were to transfer all assets in exchange for shares issued to solely him, Incorporation Relief would be available. The subsequent transfer of shares to the son, however, would be both a potentially exempt transfer (PET) for inheritance tax, and a disposal for capital gains tax purposes.

Note that Incorporation Relief effectively deducts the gain on incorporation from the base cost of the shares issued. Therefore an immediate transfer to the son would realise part of the gain deferred on incorporation. This is where Gift Relief can come to the rescue.

Gift Relief

The Gift Relief provisions were not originally intended for business incorporations. However, this route has proved to be successful and in certain cases has significant benefits over the use of Incorporation Relief. Many incorporations today use Gift Relief particularly in order to obtain the use of a tax-free loan account with the company.

The basic effect of Gift Relief is that any gains on the assets are held over against the cost of the assets to the company. For example, if a building was transferred that had a market value of £100,000, and a gain was to arise of £30,000, the company would hold the asset at a base cost of £70,000.

What Happens With This Amount 'Held Over'?

The amount held over is reduced from the cost of the asset to the company. Therefore, if the company were to subsequently dispose of the goodwill (e.g. on a disposal of the trade and assets), the proportion of the gain held over would in effect become chargeable.

Example

If Ethan had decided to incorporate his business using Gift Relief, it would be possible for him to personally retain the land and buildings which could be let to the company.

This would enable the property to be protected from creditors on a liquidation and would allow cash to be extracted from the company as rent, with no national insurance having to be paid (remember national insurance is only payable on earned income, not investment income).

The downside to the payment of rent is that Entrepreneurs Relief would then be restricted on a future disposal of the property.

Therefore it would need to be considered whether it is worthwhile charging rent given that the CGT on a future disposal of the property may then be 28% as opposed to 10%.

The goodwill would be transferred along with the trade to the company. The effect would be:

Goodwill	**£**
Market value	200,000
Cost	-
Indexation	-
Gift Relief	-200,000
Gain	NIL

BM Ltd would therefore hold the goodwill with a deemed acquisition cost of nil.

It is possible to elect to dispense with the valuing of goodwill in accordance with a Revenue and Customs statement of practice. On a straightforward gift, there would be no need to value the goodwill at incorporation as the Gift Relief claim would ensure that the company would always obtain the base cost of the transferring trader.

After April 2008, the shares in the company are likely to qualify for Entrepreneurs Relief provided the company is Ethan's 'personal company'. A personal company is a trading company where Ethan owns more than 5% of the shares and is an employee or officer of the company.

Note that where a trading asset is gifted with no disposal proceeds, any gain would be entirely deferred under Gift Relief.

However, this is unusual. Usually, an asset is partially gifted, with some disposal proceeds being received or more commonly, left outstanding on a loan account.

How this works is that you are claiming Gift Relief to 'hold over' the gain. However, because the goodwill is not actually gifted, the Gift Relief is restricted to leave an amount of gain equivalent to the disposal proceeds.

The basic theory being that gains can be fully deferred when gifted as there will be no disposal proceeds with which to pay any capital gains tax.

However, where they are part sold, there will be some disposal proceeds, and as such part of the gain will be taxable.

The disposal proceeds would then establish the loan account, which allows cash to be extracted free of tax and national insurance – the loan account is discussed shortly.

Gift Relief Procedure

The procedure that would need to be adopted is as follows:

1. A company is formed and a small number of shares would be issued for cash to the owners of the business.

2. At the date of incorporation the owners of the business enter into an agreement with the company whereby:

- The goodwill of the business is sold to the company for a nominal figure (assuming full Gift Relief is to be claimed) and
- All the other trading assets are sold at their book values.

3. The consideration for the assets transferred is satisfied wholly by cash or left on loan account. No more shares would be issued.

4. The parties sign a joint declaration to hold over any chargeable gains arising.

5. The debts of the original business are normally not transferred and would instead be collected by the original owners.

This route has a big advantage over Incorporation Relief in that a sizeable loan account can be established if some or all of the business assets are actually sold to the company for disposal proceeds (as opposed to only a nominal value). The consideration in point (3) above could be left outstanding which would form a loan account which can then be withdrawn from the company free of tax and national insurance.

It is this loan account that is advantageous to many business owners. Remember what the difference here is between Incorporation Relief and Gift Relief. Incorporation Relief applies where all the assets are gifted in exchange for shares. There will therefore be no loan account for this.

Gift Relief involves selling business assets to a company at less than market value. If the assets were sold at full value, there would be no Gift Relief, and a gain would arise. However, the loan account would then be the amount of the disposal proceeds. If you are willing to take a small capital gains tax hit now, you could therefore reap the benefits of the larger loan account later on.

Can Other Directors Use the Loan Account?

No. As the loan account is simply the disposal proceeds for the assets sold to the company, the cash would need to be extracted by the person(s) who actually sold the business.

If there is another person who is a director (for example, a spouse or adult child) one option would be for them to have their own loan account, and for this to be cleared by the disposing person's loan account. As it is a gift of cash there would be no capital gains tax implications, although for inheritance tax purposes this would be a potentially exempt transfer and, as such, provided the parent survived for at least seven years, this would be completely excluded from his estate.

Example

Peter sold the goodwill of his sole trader business to his newly formed company, Peter Limited, for £100,000 in May 2011. Peter did not claim any Gift Relief but claimed Entrepreneurs Relief.

The gain arising was £100,000. The annual CGT exemption of £10,600 reduced the taxable gain to £89,400. He would therefore pay capital gains tax of £8,940.

The company did not have the funds to pay Peter his £100,000 and therefore left this outstanding. In its accounts this would be shown as a creditor.

Peter can then use this as a way of getting cash out of the company free of tax. As the repayment of a loan this is not classed as income in his hands.

On the formation of the company, Peter's son Patrick subscribed for some shares. Peter is keen to reduce his tax charge and would like Patrick to benefit from the loan account.

One method would be for Patrick to withdraw sums from the company and, before the balance exceeds £5,000, arrange for Peter's loan account to clear Patrick's. This could either be via a book transfer (for any bookkeepers out there Dr Peter's loan account and Cr Patrick's loan account). However, care would need to be taken when considering this due to the 'company distribution' provisions and it would need to be discussed in detail with your accountant.

Valuation of Goodwill

For capital gains tax purposes, the computation is of the 'market value' of business goodwill as a separate asset.

Market value is defined in the tax legislation as being "the price which (the asset) might reasonably be expected to fetch on a sale in the open market".

Therefore, in short, goodwill is the difference between the market value of the business, less the value of any other assets that the purchaser would obtain. It is this difference that is the goodwill of the business.

There are numerous ways of valuing goodwill. One option would be to instruct a business valuer to value the business and any goodwill. You should also identify similar businesses for sale and compare their prices. Similarly, you could discount the value of future income receipts from the business using a suitable discount rate.

Many transfer agents will provide free valuation services. It would be worthwhile taking them up on this and there are numerous business and goodwill valuation software solutions that will provide a good starting point for figures.

Note that where Gift Relief is being claimed, care needs to be taken as to the order of events. The shares must be issued prior to the incorporation. This is because any amount received for the transfer of assets would reduce the availability of Gift Relief.

That's why Incorporation Relief and Gift Relief are mutually exclusive – under Incorporation Relief, the shares are issued in consideration of the transfer of assets.

Transfer of Cash in the Bank

What about any cash that is retained in the sole trader's bank account?

This could be transferred or gifted to the company. However, one option would be to retain the cash and separately loan this to the company (draw up a suitable loan agreement). This would then be added to the loan account and be extracted without a tax or national insurance charge.

Again, interest could be charged if wished which would be free of national insurance, although income tax would still be charged.

Trading Stock

Trading stock would not be subject to capital gains tax rules on a disposal.

On a transfer to the company, any charge would be under income tax. There are special provisions that deal with the transfer of stock to 'connected parties' such as your own company.

The normal connected person's rule imposes an arm's length value for the stock transferred between them, and the person incorporating the business would therefore be deemed to have disposed of the stock at market value and the company would have acquired it at market value. This could however cause substantial unrealised profits to be charged to tax on incorporation.

The tax legislation allows for an election to be made to substitute a different value as opposed to the market value. There are a number of conditions to be satisfied for a valid election, as follows:

- The arm's length value is more than the acquisition value of the stock and the price actually paid for it, and

- Both the person transferring the stock and the company make an election to Revenue and Customs. The election must be made within two tax years after the end of the chargeable period in which the trade is discontinued.

The value substituted would then be the greater of the acquisition value and the price actually received for it.

Therefore, assuming stock was transferred to the company at book value, provided the market value was in excess of this and a valid election was made and accepted by the taxman, no trading profit would arise. The company would then hold the stock at the original book value, and any profit would then be taxed in the company's hands on disposal of the stock.

The disposal consideration for the book value of the stock could be either settled in cash or left outstanding in a loan account.

Example

Patrick is transferring his business to a company. Included in the transfer will be some of the stock (widgets) of his sole trader business.

The widgets have an original cost of £5,000, but their current market value is £10,000.

Patrick is therefore looking at a potential profit of £5,000 on transfer. This would be subject to income tax and assuming he is a 40% taxpayer, income tax of £2,000 would be payable, even though he has not actually received any consideration with which to satisfy the liability.

However, Patrick would be able to transfer the widgets to the company at £5,000, and make the appropriate election.

No profit would arise on transfer, and assuming the company later sold the widgets for £10,000, the £5,000 profit would arise in the company.

16.3   INHERITANCE TAX (IHT)

In the vast majority of cases the incorporation of a business will not have any IHT implications as IHT is based on the "diminution in value" principle. This basically means that IHT applies where an individual's estate (his assets less liabilities) has reduced. In the case of incorporation, the value of shares will usually equal the value of the interest in the business transferred to the company. There will therefore be no reduction in the value of the estate and no gift arises for IHT purposes.

On the death of an individual, there is an IHT relief called Business Property Relief (BPR) that may apply so as to completely remove certain assets from the estate and from the IHT net.

It is worthwhile noting the following points in relation to BPR on incorporation:

- All shareholdings in the new company will usually qualify for 100 per cent BPR (provided the company is a trading company). Although it is required that the asset has been owned for two years, the period of ownership of the original business will be taken into account for this purpose.

- Partners who own land/buildings used by a business partnership would normally qualify for 50 per cent BPR. In the case of an individual owning such assets for the use of a company, it is only the controlling shareholder that would obtain 50 per cent BPR (although it is acceptable to combine the interests of husband and wife to determine whether either of them controls the company).

Example

John, one of the partners in the Bloggs & Co partnership, owns the partnership property which is leased to the business. The partnership pays a full market rental.

In the event of John's death, the property used by the partnership would qualify for 50 per cent BPR.

If the partnership was incorporated, and John was issued with 3,000 ordinary shares with his fellow partner receiving 7,000 shares, John would be a minority shareholder.

Assuming the property remained with John, he would not be entitled to any Business Property Relief were he to die whilst still owning the asset.

16.4   VAT

The general rule is that the disposal of goods forming part of the assets of a business is a supply made in the course of the business and therefore VAT will be chargeable on the sale of fixtures, fittings, plant and machinery and stock. HMRC also treats disposals of goodwill as taxable supplies.

However, there is one key relief available which applies where the transfer of the business is a "transfer of a going concern". The conditions required to be satisfied are:

- There is a transfer of a business or a part of a business capable of separate operation.

- The transfer must be of a going concern (TOGC), in other words, there must be no significant break in trading.

- The transferee must carry on the same kind of business as the transferor.

- The transferee must already be or must become a VAT registered trader.

- It should also be noted that there are special provisions that apply to TOGC treatment where a property that is being transferred is a supply subject to VAT.

- Where the ownership of the business is transferred to the company, it is possible for the trader and company to jointly apply on VAT Form 68 for the company to take over the transferor's original VAT registration, provided that:

o   The registration of the original business is to be cancelled from the date of the transfer.

o   The new business is not already registered, but is liable or entitled to be registered.

The effect of a successful application would be that the company stands in the shoes of the transferor and would therefore take over the VAT rights and obligations of the transferor.

16.5   STAMP DUTY

If any land or property is to be transferred to the company, the Stamp Duty Land Tax (SDLT) implications will need to be considered.

On residential property the rates for purchases are:

Consideration	%
Up to £125,000	0
More than £125,000 and up to £250,000	1
More than £250,000 and up to £500,000	3
More than £500,000 and up to £1,000,000	4
More than £1,000,000	5

There is also a special 0% rate for first-time buyers on properties costing up to £250,000.

On non-residential property the rates for purchases are:

Consideration	%
Up to £150,000	0
More than £150,000 and up to £250,000	1
More than £250,000 and up to £500,000	3
More than £500,000	4

The exemption for non-residential property with a value of up to £150,000 is a useful addition, and will exempt many small businesses who wish to transfer their business premises, although it is fair to say that stamp duty would not have been a key consideration – the corporation tax and capital gains tax implications are arguably the most important.

Many of the changes are really just a case of bringing stamp duty into the 21st century.

The appeals procedure has been changed and brought more into line with income tax and capital gains tax. In particular, SDLT is a tax on transactions as opposed to documents, reducing opportunities to avoid the tax charge.

If you plan to transfer the lease of your business premises, you should take professional advice, as there are some complex provisions regarding the SDLT charge on leases.

There is an exemption from stamp duty on the sale or transfer of goodwill upon incorporation, in respect of documents executed after 22 April 2002.

This makes the sale of goodwill to a company upon incorporation (as opposed to a gift) potentially more attractive. The sale proceeds could be left outstanding as a loan to the company, and withdrawn without further tax consequences.

In the past, debtors used to often be retained by the sole trader in order to avoid stamp duty. However, stamp duty is no longer charged on the transfer of debtors, and they could therefore be transferred to the company.

Even if they were transferred note that the receipt of money from a debtor would not usually be charged to tax. Under the accruals basis of accounting, the sale will have already been recorded and taxed in the sole trader's accounts (Dr Debtors, Cr Sales). The receipt of cash by the company would then not impact on the profit and loss account, being only a balance sheet transaction (Dr Cash, Cr Debtors).

Chapter 17

Incorporation Checklist

The precise procedures to follow when setting up a company will depend to a large extent on the particular trade/business you are undertaking.

As a guide the following actions should be taken:

- Check that no trade rules prohibit you trading as a limited company.

- Consider the timing of incorporation. In particular, if cash flow is important note that the date of cessation can impact heavily on the final income tax assessments.

- Consider:

  1. The value of goodwill.
  2. Whether and how to avoid capital gains tax.
  3. Shareholdings, appointing directors and company secretary.
  4. What assets are to go into the company.

- Once you've formed the company and have the company number:

  1. Open a new bank account.
  2. Consider VAT registration or transfer of registration.
  3. Get new stationery.

- Consider whether to have a formal sale document or just heads of agreement.

- Consider VAT implications - is there a transfer of a going concern?

- Draw up sales agreement and if necessary get it stamped.

- Inform everyone concerned (customers, suppliers, the taxman).

- Put any legal transfer of land and buildings into motion.

- Commence trading in company name.

- If you used holdover relief to avoid capital gains tax on goodwill, submit holdover relief claim.

- Set up new accounting system.

- When submitting tax returns, do not forget cessation rules or CGT computations.

Chapter 18

Transferring a Business Out of a Company

We've looked at length at the tax implications of transferring your business into a company. But what happens if you change your mind and decide to go back to running your business as a sole trader or partnership?

Well for tax purposes this is known as 'disincorporation' and the first thing you should note is that the tax position on transferring assets out of a company is much less favourable than transferring assets into a company.

18.1 TRANSFERRING YOUR BUSINESS

We looked in Chapter 13 at some of the occasions when it may actually reduce your tax bill to carry out your business as a sole trader or partnership as opposed to using a limited company.

If after incorporating your business you decide some years down the line that you want to trade personally again, you will need to transfer the business out of the company.

This involves a transfer of the assets of the business so you would need to look at each element of your business and consider the tax impact.

You'd usually be looking at transferring:

- Goodwill
- Land/Property
- Stock
- Creditors/Debtors/Cash

The main tax problem with disincorporation is that there are very few tax reliefs or concessions available. The two key problems will be capital gains tax and income tax.

18.2   CAPITAL GAINS TAX

The transfer of assets from the company to shareholders would be a disposal for capital gains tax purposes. As the shareholders and company would be connected, the disposal proceeds would be deemed to be the market value, irrespective of the actual amount the assets are transferred for.

So the company would need to obtain a valuation of any assets transferred and the transfer would crystallise a capital gain based on the uplift in value from the original acquisition.

Frequently this will be a big problem with respect to the company's goodwill. It is also important to note that goodwill can exist even if no value is reflected on the balance sheet. Even if a value is shown on the balance sheet the actual market value may be much higher.

The company would then be taxed on any capital gain on the goodwill transferred at its marginal rate of corporation tax.

The original method of incorporation could also be relevant here. For instance if when the original business was transferred to the company a Gift Relief claim was made any gain on the goodwill on incorporation may have been deferred.

This would then reduce the base cost of the asset held in the company. So a subsequent transfer of the asset back to the company would crystallise the original 'deferred gain' as well as any subsequent uplift in value.

Unlike when you transfer a business to a company you can't claim Gift Relief when transferring assets out of a company.

Example

Jack runs his business as a sole trader. The only asset is goodwill valued at £200,000. He decides to incorporate and he transfers the goodwill to the company. He also claims Gift Relief to hold over any capital gain.

His CGT calculation on incorporation is as follows:

Goodwill	£
Market value	200,000
Cost	-
Indexation	-
Gift Relief	-200,000
Gain	NIL

Five years later he decides he wants to transfer his business back into his own name. The goodwill is now valued at £500,000.

The transfer of the goodwill from the company to Jack is a disposal for capital gains purposes by the company. However, the base cost of the goodwill in the company is NIL. This is the £200,000 value of the goodwill at incorporation, less the Gift Relief claimed.

This means that the full value of £500,000 would be charged as a capital gain in the company when it is transferred back to Jack.

If Jack had chosen the Incorporation Relief method when he incorporated his business, the £200,000 gain would have been held over against the cost of the shares not the cost of the goodwill in the company. As such a transfer of the goodwill back into his name would have only crystallised a capital gain of £300,000. This is because the base cost of the goodwill would be £200,000 and not NIL.

The CGT charge on assets transferred back to you will probably be the main tax problem when you disincorporate.

If there has been a substantial uplift in the value of property or goodwill you could find the company is left with a large corporation tax charge on the capital gain.

Of course this will depend on the market value of the assets in the company. Many have seen property and business/goodwill values decline in the current economic climate. In this case now may be a good time to disincorporate with minimal capital gain exposure.

18.3   INCOME TAX

The other big problem with transferring your business into your own name is that there may well be an income tax charge on you personally.

You and the company are treated as completely separate for tax purposes. So if the company transfers any assets to shareholders the company would expect to receive proceeds worth the full value of that asset. If it doesn't, this will be classed as a distribution to the shareholders. Essentially this is taxed as a dividend to the shareholders as they've extracted value from the company.

This treatment can apply whenever the company does not receive the full value from an asset transferred to shareholders.

Therefore if you simply transfer goodwill from a company into your name not only would there be a disposal by the company for capital gains purposes, but you would be subject to an income tax charge.

If you paid the company for the goodwill it would only be the difference between the market value and the amount you paid that could be subject to income tax.

Example

If Jack from the previous example paid the company £400,000 for the goodwill he would be classed as receiving a distribution of £100,000 from the company.

There is also a danger that any transfer of assets to director/shareholders by the company could be subject to the 'benefit in kind' rules with the result that income tax and national insurance could become payable.

Of course, if you did pay the company the full market value for any assets transferred to you this would avoid any income tax charge. The company would then hold the cash proceeds and you would still have the problem of extracting the cash tax efficiently.

Some options could include:

- Becoming non-UK resident and extracting cash as a dividend free of income tax.

- Extracting cash over the course of a number of tax years to utilise your basic-rate tax band. This would allow cash to be extracted free of income tax.

- You could simply use the cash in the company to undertake a new business activity (e.g., a new trade or investment business).

- The company could be wound up and the cash extracted as a capital distribution (and therefore subject to CGT at up to 28% or even less if Entrepreneurs Relief applies).

18.4   OTHER IMPLICATIONS

As well as the CGT and potential income tax charge there are other tax implications of transferring your business from your company into your own name.

Many of these apply because the company will be classed as ceasing to trade.

On the plus side trading stock and debtors can generally be transferred free of tax.

However, if there are any loans made to the directors ensure these are repaid to prevent a benefit in kind tax charge arising.

You also need to be very careful over the allocation of any trading losses in the company. These can in general only be offset against income of the company before it is wound up (although in some instances may be offset against trading profits of the preceding 36 months).

Make sure that trading losses are utilised in the period before disincorporation as they'll be lost after the trade has been transferred. So for instance any assets which may realise a capital gain should be sold before disincorporation if the company has made trading losses in the same accounting period.

Example

BBH Ltd had trading losses of £1 million in the accounting period ended 31 December 2010 and £500,000 in the six months to 30 June 2011. It transferred its trade to the sole shareholder, Bill, on 30 June 2011.

It sold assets on 2 September 2011 which crystallised a capital gain of £400,000.

The trading losses in the company are effectively lost and cannot be offset against the capital gain of £400,000. If BBH had sold the assets on 2 June 2011 the £500,000 loss could have been offset against the gain and it would have avoided a corporation tax charge.

Note that the losses won't even be carried forward as they are only carried forward in the company for offset against profits of the same trade (which is now no longer in the company).

18.5 WINDING UP THE COMPANY & EXTRACTING CASH

Following the transfer of the trade, any surplus profits remaining within the company will need to be distributed to the shareholders.

There are two main ways that you can extract cash from the company.

Firstly you could wind up the company and extract any cash as a capital distribution. Alternatively you could simply extract the cash as a dividend.

Liquidating the Company

Liquidation itself can be a lengthy and complex procedure. However a Revenue extra statutory concession, *ESC C16*, can make this process easier.

This states that where a distribution is paid by a company prior to a striking off under the Companies Act, it can be treated as a capital distribution (as akin to the company being formally wound up).

This is a much simpler and cheaper route than opting for a formal liquidation of the company and is probably something that many readers should consider.

If you are UK resident when you wind up the company the advantage of this is that capital gains tax (CGT) applies as opposed to income tax. On the distribution of the cash to the shareholders, this would result in a gain for the shareholders, based on their ownership of the shares.

The key relief here will be Entrepreneurs Relief. If the shareholders are entitled to claim this, they could see their effective CGT rate reduced to 10%

Therefore a winding up could entitle you to a lower rate of tax on the cash receipt. It would be essential to consider whether the company will qualify for Entrepreneurs Relief as well as the size of the gain and availability of the annual CGT exemption.

Note that draft legislation has been published that seeks to give the ESC C16 relief a statutory footing from April 2011. However, the new provisions will only apply capital treatment to a distribution if it is less than £4,000.

If the draft legislation is enacted, business owners who want to extract larger amounts as capital will therefore need to formally liquidate the company.

Dividend Extraction

The alternative would be to extract the cash as a dividend. You'll suffer tax on the dividend at 25% if you are a higher-rate taxpayer, rising to 36.1% if your income is above £150,000. If you are a basic-rate taxpayer you could receive it tax free.

For most higher-rate and additional-rate taxpayers there will therefore be a substantial benefit in opting for the capital distribution treatment above, particularly if Entrepreneurs Relief applies.

This is not to say that capital treatment is always beneficial. If, for example, you had income tax losses, substantial tax credits (e.g., EIS income tax credits), were a basic rate taxpayer or were planning on leaving the UK, you may want to opt for a dividend.

Chapter 19

Offshore Tax Planning

Although not directly relevant to many of those considering incorporating a business, it's worthwhile giving an overview of the various offshore tax rules.

The first point to note when looking at overseas tax planning is that it is *residence* that is all important. Both companies and individuals have residence in one or more countries and it is this residence that primarily determines liability to UK taxes.

A company is regarded as a UK resident if:

• It is a UK incorporated company, or
• Its *central management and control* is in the UK.

Therefore, where a UK-registered company is used, the company would automatically be UK resident. The effect of this is that it is subject to UK corporation tax on its worldwide income and gains.

By contrast, an offshore company that is centrally managed and controlled from overseas would only be subject to UK corporation tax on its UK income. Any overseas income and all gains would be outside the scope of UK corporation tax. (Note that gains arising from assets used in a UK trade would still be subject to UK corporation tax.)

Some people try and live in the UK, yet argue that the central management and control of their company is undertaken overseas. Various legal cases, including the case of Wood v Holden in 2005 have indicated that of crucial importance is where the board of directors meet. Provided the board actually gives proper consideration to any transactions the company undertakes and does not, for example, simply rubber stamp decisions already taken by a UK resident shareholder, the central management and control could be established overseas.

The risk though is that proper procedures may not be followed and in such cases HMRC may argue that the company is run by the controlling shareholder in the UK. In these circumstances the company would be classed as UK resident and subject to UK corporation tax.

As far as individuals are concerned, there is considerable uncertainty over the definition of 'residence'. HMRC's practice has been to regard you as resident in the UK during a tax year if:

- You spend 183 days or more in the UK during the tax year, or

- Although here for less than 183 days, you spent more than 90 days per year in the country in the past three years (on average). You will then be classed as UK resident from the fourth year.

These requirements are not set in stone and recent decisions of the Courts and Commissioners' as well as HMRC guidance have made it clear that these 'tests' are not conclusive. If you are in the UK for, say, 80 days per tax year, own a house here and your family live here, the taxman may argue that you remain UK resident. It would therefore be advisable to establish your 'home' overseas and minimise UK visits if you are trying to argue non-UK residence status.

Note that for capital gains tax purposes, there are special provisions that may require you to remain overseas for at least five tax years to avoid UK capital gains tax.

UK resident individuals are subject to UK income tax and capital gains tax on their worldwide income and gains, whereas non-resident individuals are only subject to UK income tax on their UK income and gains arising from assets used in a UK trade.

19.1   HOW DO OFFSHORE ISSUES AFFECT YOU?

There are plenty of ways that the offshore dimension could affect your tax planning.

1) Let's say you want to dispose of a UK business. Could you become non-resident to avoid UK capital gains tax?

Wrong! The disposal would continue to be within the charge to UK capital gains tax, as the various assets disposed of would be classed as part of a UK trade.

A method to side-step this would be to incorporate your business. By transferring your business to a company, you now own the shares in the company, and the company owns the business.

You could then become non-resident and dispose of the shares, as opposed to the assets. Provided the purchaser has no objection, and you satisfy the various non-residency requirements, your disposal should be exempt from UK capital gains tax, as a disposal of an asset which is not used in a UK trade.

2) What about incorporating your business into an offshore company?

This would be fine provided the company was within the charge to UK corporation tax (i.e., UK resident). If you argued that the company was non-resident and outside the scope of UK capital gains tax HMRC would not be too happy about allowing a deferral of gains on incorporation where a future disposal would be outside the scope of UK tax. Therefore Gift Relief would be restricted.

3) What if you went to live overseas – any opportunities there?

If you became non-resident, this opens up more options to minimise UK tax.

You could pay yourself dividends from your UK company, effectively free of UK income tax, as any higher rate tax is restricted and the notional tax credit is deemed to satisfy any basic rate liability. This could be a useful mechanism for extracting cash from the company – build up funds in the company over a number of years and pay a large dividend during the tax year of non-residence, free of UK income tax!

(Note there would be other additional implications to consider here.)

When compared to an unincorporated business, this looks very favourable, as profits from a UK trade would be fully charged to UK income tax, just as for a UK-resident individual.

However, when using a company, although corporation tax is still payable by the company, this is significantly less than the income tax charge for a sole trader/partner, and no personal tax liability!

19.2   UK RESIDENTS USING OFFSHORE COMPANIES

There are typically two main objectives when an individual forms an offshore company.

*   Tax savings
*   Privacy

These objectives are pretty universal and most offshore incorporators will have one or more of these objectives in mind. You'll frequently see websites offering offshore structures as the answer to all your financial problems. However, what about if you are a UK resident?

Does the UK simply allow you to simply form an offshore company and transfer your cash/assets to this to escape your UK tax and other legal responsibilities?

Well, the answer is a resounding no. That's why you need to tread carefully particularly when you see the countless websites promoting the benefits of offshore companies/trusts and bank accounts.

It's all very well income or assets being tax exempt overseas, but if you're a UK resident, the UK taxman will want a slice of your worldwide income, wherever it's earned and whatever you do with it.

The UK angle is therefore paramount and, in actual fact, the UK position should be considered first before the overseas position. If your overseas income or the income of your wholly owned company is going to be taxed in the UK, any proposed tax savings overseas will usually go out of the window.

So what exactly does the UK allow or not? Well let's have a look at the above reasons for establishing an offshore structure, and see what the position is if you live and work in the UK.

Firstly, there is the tax-planning perspective.

19.3   TAX PLANNING

The main objective is often to avoid taxes. There are a number of different mechanisms by which an offshore company could be used to avoid taxes. It may simply be that income earned in the UK is transferred overseas and grows tax free in an offshore company – often known as an offshore international business corporation (IBC).

Alternatively, an individual could actually be trading and using the offshore IBC to siphon profits offshore. They could, for example, be using a wholly owned offshore IBC as a recharging company to charge their UK trading company for services.

In terms of capital gains, using an offshore company would be tremendously beneficial, as a non-resident company would not be subject to UK tax on any gains made (for example, on disposal of UK property).

You'll see that the theoretical possibilities are endless – that's why the UK has some pretty restrictive rules to prevent many of the above, and that's why you shouldn't believe a lot of the general info on the web that fails to take account of these.

Each of these is a complex area in itself, but let's take a quick look at some of the ways the UK taxman will stop the above:

Company Residence

As you've seen the UK taxman can argue that any company, no matter where it is established, is UK resident if its central management and control is in the UK.

The impact of being UK resident is, in most cases, enough to prevent most offshore schemes from achieving their objectives as the company would be charged to UK corporation tax on its worldwide profits.

So if you're a UK resident individual, simply using an offshore company to hold offshore assets or conduct an offshore trading operation would not avoid UK taxes, as the company would be likely to be taxed on any income.

Of course the crucial aspect is whether the company is managed or controlled from the UK. If you're a UK resident shareholder it's usually pretty difficult to argue that the company is not controlled in the UK, particularly for a trading company.

As a minimum, you'd probably need to use offshore nominees and an overseas intermediary entity such as an offshore trust or foundation to actually own the shares in the company. This would then at least allow the possibility of arguing that you didn't actually control the company. This would need to be borne out by the facts, and you'd need to ensure that the trustees or overseas directors did actually control the company.

Therefore simply using an offshore company in itself is not enough to avoid UK taxes.

Apportionment of Gains

As well as the company residence issue, the taxman also has another weapon in his arsenal. If a UK resident is a shareholder in an offshore company (and owns more than 10 per cent of the shares) the gains of the non-resident company can be apportioned to the UK resident. So if you owned 30 per cent of an offshore company and the company sold a property realising a gain of £100,000, HMRC could tax you on a gain of £30,000.

This can catch a lot of transactions but crucially it will catch UK residents who try and use an offshore company to hold UK property. Of course non-residents (companies and individuals) are not subject to UK tax on gains arising. It's therefore tempting for a UK resident to use an offshore non-resident company (that manages to get around the central management and control test) to hold investment property. This provision should, in most cases, ensure that UK tax is not avoided on the gains.

Apportionment from Offshore Trusts

Using offshore trusts is just as popular as using offshore companies, and for this reason there are avoidance provisions similar to those above. Essentially again UK residents will be allocated gains of offshore trusts where they receive capital receipts from the trust. So if an offshore trust realises a gain on a property disposal of, say, £300,000 and then gives a UK resident beneficiary a distribution from the trust of, say, £100,000, that £100,000 could be assessed as a gain of the UK resident.

Attribution of Gains When You Set Up a Trust

There are separate and specific provisions to allocate gains that arise to offshore trusts to UK resident settlors (again if you're also a UK domiciliary). Basically this applies to where you set up an offshore trust and transfer the funds or assets to the trust. The gains of the trust can then be taxed as yours.

Transfer of Assets Abroad

There is some pretty wide-ranging legislation that can apply to anyone who transfers assets overseas. This is targeted more at income tax avoidance and applies to UK residents (and UK domiciliaries) who transfer assets overseas. The income and any benefits obtained from the transfer can be taxed on the UK resident. There is an exemption under this section for transfers that are made for bona fide commercial reasons. So provided you have a sound reason for the transfer you should be OK.

How Can UK Residents Use Offshore Structures?

Non-UK domiciliaries can make use of the remittance basis and are still best placed to take advantage of offshore opportunities. This means they are only taxed on overseas income and gains to the extent that they are actually brought into the UK.

As from 6 April 2008 there are however a number of changes that have been made to claiming this special tax treatment. Most notably any non UK domiciliaries that have been UK resident for more than 7 of the past 10 tax years would need to pay an annual charge of £30,000 for the privilege of claiming the remittance basis.

Nevertheless where they are excluded from the £30,000 tax charge or if they have substantial overseas income they can take advantage of offshore structures to reduce UK tax.

If you're a UK resident and a UK domiciliary your opportunities to avoid tax by using an offshore structure are more limited. Unless you spread ownership pretty thinly using it to hold UK investment property and avoiding CGT is pretty much out of the question.

The main opportunity would arise in avoiding UK tax on overseas income, especially trading income, although this in itself is not straightforward as HMRC can argue that any company is UK resident, as well as using the transfer of assets provisions.

Provided you establish commercially viable entities overseas and use a solid structure such as an offshore trust combined with an offshore company you could get some of the benefits.

What won't work, however, is simply setting up an offshore company to avoid tax on UK assets.

As always, taking some sound advice is pretty important given the range of the offshore tax provisions.

Can You Transfer a UK Company Overseas?

This is an issue many UK business owners ask about. Unfortunately the position is not straightforward. If the company is UK incorporated you can't transfer it overseas. Because it is UK incorporated it will remain UK resident even if controlled from overseas (for example, even if the shares are transferred to an offshore trust or if you as the shareholder are non-UK resident, the company itself would still fall inside the UK tax net).

The sole exception to this is if you can use a double tax treaty to gain treaty residence overseas. We look at the use of double tax treaties in our offshore tax guide *Non Resident & Offshore Tax Planning*.

If you want to use an overseas company you would usually need to incorporate an offshore company and transfer funds into it. This would not be beneficial for existing assets held in the UK company, as any transfer to the overseas company could crystallize a tax charge.

However, establishing an overseas company could be beneficial if you are planning to set up a new operation, particularly if it involves an overseas trade or investment. The most straightforward way to achieve this would be to incorporate the offshore company as a subsidiary of the UK company. Funds could then be transferred by way of a combination of share capital and intercompany loans (at market interest rates).

There are a few hurdles that would need to be overcome. Firstly, as stated above, you'd need to ensure that the control of the company was overseas. This would usually be achieved by having an overseas board of directors actually running the company, with the UK company acting purely as a shareholder. Note if you were a UK resident you would not be able to exercise control over the company's activities and still argue it was non-resident.

The second 'hurdle' would be the controlled foreign companies (CFC) legislation. This is a complex area of law but can apportion profits of the overseas tax haven subsidiary to the UK company (where they would be subject to UK tax) where various conditions are satisfied. There are however some exemptions that you may be able to take advantage of to prevent the apportionment. These rules are currently being comprehensively updated.

If you were successful in this any profits generated by the overseas subsidiary would not be subject to UK tax. Provided you established the company in a no tax jurisdiction such as Panama, the Bahamas, Nevis or the Cayman Islands there would be no tax levied on the company.

Another aspect to be considered would be the tax regime in the country where you are investing. It's unlikely there will be a tax treaty in place if you are trading from a tax haven.

19.4   PRIVACY

Another main reason for using offshore structures is privacy. While I think it's important that you should be able to keep your info away from prying eyes, you need to make a distinction here between hiding cash or assets from the taxman and hiding your wealth from third parties.

Obviously you should never use an offshore structure to hide assets from the taxman. If you're ever found out there will be some pretty substantial penalties along with interest.

Now we've got that out of the way, you can use an offshore structure to improve financial privacy in a number of ways including:

- Numbered accounts with no name mentioned.
- Bearer shares with share ownership represented by physical ownership of share certificates.
- Use of nominees to own shares.
- Using different jurisdictions for the incorporation of the offshore company trust, its bank account and the nominee directors.
- Using countries that don't have public share registers.
- Using countries that don't have exchange of information agreements and/or are traditionally extra strong on client confidentiality.
- Using a network of offshore IBCs to channel funds through.
- Using offshore foundations that limit your control over the offshore structure's assets.

Therefore you can still use offshore opportunities to make assets more difficult to find by any outsiders, although whether you would want to be (or should be) doing that is another question.

You should also bear in mind that after the 2009 G20 summit there are likely to be many more 'exchange of information treaties' signed. These allow information to be passed between different countries much more easily.

For a more detailed look at the offshore opportunities available, see our publications *Non-Resident & Offshore Tax Planning* or *The World's Best Tax Havens* available from the Taxcafe.co.uk website.

Chapter 20

Conclusion

There are a number of issues to consider on the incorporation of a business, including, both taxation and commercial implications.

The initial step should be to consider whether there are any advantages to be gained from incorporation. The use of salaries/dividends and directors' loan accounts should be carefully evaluated against the likely profitability of the company.

Once a decision to incorporate has been made, the question then is how to incorporate and to ensure that the deferral reliefs are obtained. The structure of an incorporation will usually be driven by the vendor's requirements in the context of these reliefs. In recent years, the Gift Relief route has often been preferred as it can secure significant stamp duty savings and can facilitate the creation of a loan account in the purchase company that can be repaid tax free.

Please note that the issues contained in this guide are intended for guidance only and professional advice should always be taken with regard to your particular circumstances.